First

11/22 £1

GIBRALTAR

EXPERIENCE IN THE 1960s

AND

FOUND OUT

Best wishes from the author

C. R. TOYE

January 2018

Gibraltar

Experience in the 1960s

and

Found Out

C RICHARD TOYE

GREAT WESTERN BOOKS

Copyright © C Richard Toye 2017
First published in 2017 by Great Western Books
38 Abden Avenue, Kinghorn, Fife, Scotland, KY3 9TE
www.amolibros.co.uk

Distributed by Gardners Books, 1 Whittle Drive, Eastbourne,
East Sussex, BN23 6QH
Tel: +44(0)1323 521555 | Fax: +44(0)1323 521666

British Library Cataloguing in Publication Data
A catalogue record for this book is available from the British
Library.

ISBN 978-0-9543711-2-8

Typeset by Amolibros, Milverton, Somerset
This book production has been managed by Amolibros
Printed and bound by T J International Ltd, Padstow,
Cornwall, UK

The Author

Born in Plymouth, Devon, Charles Toye did a shipwright apprenticeship in Devonport and Rosyth Dockyards. He was in numerous managerial posts for the Ministry of Defence, one of which included a tour of duty in Gibraltar. He studied at Strathclyde University and gained a First Class Honours degree in Naval Architecture.

After two years as a marine surveyor for the Board of Trade in Belfast –from 1969-1971 in troubled times – he returned to the MOD as a Naval Constructor at Rosyth Dockyard followed by duty at Swan Hunters Newcastle and finally at Rosyth Dockyard.

He is retired and lives with his family in Kinghorn, Fife, Scotland.

Previously published:

Sandy: the true story of a boy and his friends growing up in Cornwall in the late 1800s.

Mysteries of the Ladybank Woods

Acknowledgements

My thanks to Anne Weatherston who spent many hours typing and re-typing my manuscript. And to Jo, my sister-in-law who gave me the spark to start writing about my experiences in Gibraltar in the 1960s.

This book is dedicated to my wife Margaret

GIBRALTAR

Gibraltar experience in the sixties

'Barbary Apes – the only wild monkeys in Europe.'

'The Barbary Apes have roamed the Rock for hundreds of years and were long a symbol of the British presence in Gibraltar.

'There was a saying that if the Barbary Apes on the Rock died out then the British would lose Gibraltar. As the existing apes on the Rock showed signs of diminishing in numbers, a pack of Barbary Apes were captured on the Atlas Mountains in North Africa and resettled on the Rock. Since that time both packs of apes have prospered!'

While working for the Ministry of Defence in Scotland I was transferred in 1962 to an overseeing post in Newcastle upon Tyne. There I was employed as a Constructive Overseer on the build of minesweepers for the Australian Navy.

After working in Newcastle for several months I noticed in the main office an MOD circular advertising for an

Assistant Manager to work in Gibraltar for a tour of three years. Knowing that the allowances during this tour were quite good financially I applied for the post.

Many weeks had gone by since I had applied for the job and I had given up on the chance of being chosen for the post. So I was surprised one morning on going into the main office in Newcastle to be called to see the Principal Overseer. I was wondering if I had done something wrong in my overseeing duties.

In trepidation I knocked on the Principal's office door; I nearly jumped out of my skin when I heard the Principal shout loudly for me to enter.

The Principal asked me to sit down. On his desk he lifted an official document from a tray and then looked at me.

In his usual loud voice he said he had a reply about my application for a tour abroad and I had been successful. Did I want to take up the post in Malta?

Now I was confused as I knew that I had applied for the job in Gibraltar Dockyard. "Excuse me," I said, "but I thought the job was in Gibraltar."

The Principal was now confused, I think, knowing he had made a mistake by saying Malta instead of Gibraltar. To overcome his embarrassment he growled, "Do you want the job or not?"

I replied that it didn't matter if it was Malta or Gibraltar I would take the job. I knew both would be attractive places financially and had warm climates.

That evening I went home quite buoyant as I knew the post would give my family and myself a better living in a sunny climate for three years.

On hearing the news of the Gibraltar post my wife

Margaret was quite excited about spending three years abroad. Since moving from Dunfermline we had been living a humdrum life. With my low income it meant we couldn't afford many luxuries and had a limited social life.

Within a few days I had confirmation in writing that I had the Gibraltar post as an Assistant Manager in the Constructive Division of the dockyard. This allowed my wife and I to make plans for the move and we were able to put our house up for sale.

I was given an advance allowance so we exchanged our Reliant Robin for a brand new Morris Traveller. The Morris car was a joy to drive compared to the austerity and bumpy ride of the three-wheeler car.

On the following Monday I managed to get time off from the office so that my wife and I could visit a solicitor and put our house up for sale.

During the next two weeks after our house was advertised for sale we didn't have many viewers of the property. Those viewers who did look at our house didn't seem very interested.

On the second Saturday we had a visit from a well dressed man who looked about thirty years old. He introduced himself as Bill McFarlane and he was representing his father's firm, a meat exporter in Aberdeenshire. The firm was looking for a house for one of their salesmen who would operate in the Newcastle area. Mr McFarlane was well spoken with an Aberdeenshire accent, so to us he seemed quite genuine.

The paperwork and brochures he laid on a table after he entered our house showed that he had visited the Agricultural Show that had been held on the 'Moor' in Newcastle during that week.

He looked around the house and was most thorough in his examination of the rooms and garden. When he was finished, to our surprise, he said that he was interested in buying the house and would pay the full price we asked for without any haggling.

He wrote out an offer for purchase of the property on one of his firm's headed blank notepaper.

With the sale we thought concluded my wife set out some biscuits and a cup of coffee for Mr McFarlane. While he was drinking his coffee he asked me if I could loan him £10. He explained that he was staying at the Turk's Head hotel in Newcastle and had forgotten to draw money from the bank on the previous day and had left himself short.

I was tempted to let him have the money as I thought we had such a good offer for the house. I held back as at the time we were not well off and had very little spare money. Instead I suggested that he ask the manager at his hotel for a loan.

Mr McFarlane's request for money made us suspicious, but we soon forgot about it with our thoughts turning to more immediate things which were the arrangements for our move to Gibraltar.

On the following Monday I visited our solicitor and handed to him Mr McFarlane's letter that stated the details for the purchase of our house. This done I contacted Hoults Ltd to arrange the pick-up and storage of our furniture for the next three years.

All went well with arrangements with the move until about a week later the solicitor selling our house rang me. He explained that as he had not received a legal confirmation of the proposed purchase of our house from

Mr McFarlane's solicitor he felt he had to make direct contact with Mr McFarlane's father.

So he rang the telephone number quoted on Mr McFarlane's letter of intent of purchase. The telephone was answered by the owner of the meat export firm. When the subject of the purchase of our house was raised, the real Mr McFarlane said he didn't know anything about it.

When the solicitor suggested that it was his son who had made the offer Mr McFarlane was quite irate and said his only son was seven years old and slammed down the telephone.

The solicitor after explaining this embarrassing turn of events said, "It looks as if you have been tricked by a confidence trickster and there is no sale." I thanked him and asked him to send on his bill. I concluded in saying that with little time left before we moved to Gibraltar we had to contact an estate agent to arrange for the house to be rented unfurnished for three years.

The next day I visited an estate agent in Newcastle and arranged for our house to be advertised for rental for three years.

With the rental arrangements concluded I contacted the firm Hoults and fixed a date for the pick-up and storage of our furniture.

By the end of that week I received our tickets for the flight from Gatwick to Gibraltar on 20th August.

We were now free to contact our relations and friends in Scotland so that we could visit them before leaving for Gibraltar. There was a problem with our visit to Scotland as I had to take our new car early to an agent so that its shipment to Gibraltar could be arranged.

This meant we had to hire a car for our trip to Scotland,

so we visited the sales office who sold us our car and asked if they could fix up a hire of a car for one week.

The salesman, after checking other businesses, said that because of the holiday period all the hire cars had been taken. The only car he could obtain for us was a 1938, 14-horsepower Wolsey belonging to one of their clients.

Although the car was twenty-four years old it had been regularly serviced and kept in a good condition by the client, a woman who'd had the car from when it was new.

The salesman said she would allow us to hire her car for £10 to help us out, but expected us to take good care of it. He finally warned us that the car would only do seventeen miles to the gallon.

We were relieved to have the car for our trip as we didn't fancy travelling to the various destinations in Scotland with an eighteen-month-old daughter by train and bus.

That weekend we collected the Wolsey in the Newcastle saleroom. We found the car in immaculate condition, but it was like a wartime armoured car with high sides and its seats perched high up. It had a high curved back with a pull-down flap covering the baggage space.

The signalling indicators were quite antiquated as they were in the shape of levers that operated from the door frames. The levers had yellow plastic covers so that they could be seen at a distance. The windscreen wipers were made up of an array of arms that looked quite fragile.

Looking at the car I had to smile as it reminded me of the cars used by the Al Capone gang during the prohibition period in America.

When I brought the old Wolsey home my wife Margaret burst out laughing when she saw the old-styled car. She said, "It will have to do but I hope it won't break down on our way to Scotland."

When loading up the car we found that it had plenty of room and was reasonably comfortable inside despite the seats being high up in the car.

We set off on the Saturday morning with the weather fine and dry. I kept to a speed of about forty m.p.h. in case the engine conked out.

As we reached the English/Scottish border it started to rain. For a while the windscreen wipers worked but as the rain became heavier they stopped operating. So to overcome this fault we had to work the wipers by hand thus causing me to go even slower.

To add to our problems the direction indicators wouldn't work unless we banged the side of the car to loosen them from their mounting.

Despite the weather and the problems with the car, we arrived in Dunfermline to stay with our friends, the Pollocks, quite late in the day.

Our stay was quite an enjoyable one and we visited a number of beauty spots in Fife and Perthshire with our friends and the old car stood up well to the long journeys.

We always got looks from passers-by as we trundled through the numerous villages en route. Although we didn't have any major breakdowns I felt I was filling up the petrol tank at every other filling station.

On our return to Dunfermline we said our farewells to the Pollocks and headed off to Glasgow to stay with Margaret's mum and dad.

Again the trip across to Glasgow was quite slow as beside the car having its usual problems with windscreen wipers and indicators, the condition of the roads was not of a high standard. We had to take the country roads out of Fife and cross the Forth river by the old Kincardine bridge. The Forth Road Bridge at North Queensferry was just being built at that time. After a tiring journey we reached Margaret's old home safe and sound.

Margaret's family were overjoyed to see us and made a lot of our daughter Louise.

During the week we were in Glasgow we made short trips to see Margaret's sister Betty and her family as well as visits to other relatives.

The time we spent with the family seemed to fly by so with our flight to Gibraltar due in a few days time we had to say our farewell to the family and head back to Newcastle.

Margaret's mum and dad were quite upset with our move to Gibraltar as they didn't expect to see us for three years. To soften the thoughts of our long absence we insisted that Margaret's Mum and Dad came out to Gibraltar and stay with us for a holiday once we had suitable accommodation. Although they agreed, it would be a tall order for them as they had never been abroad before or flown in an aeroplane.

This was not unusual for many families in Scotland as chartered holidays didn't exist and people mainly holidayed in England or other parts of Scotland.

On our return to Newcastle we returned the car in one piece to the saleroom and went to bed quite early after the long journey.

The next day we finished off the last of our packing for our move to Gibraltar. A couple of days later we said our farewells to our relatives and friends in Newcastle. The following day we travelled to London and then on to

Gatwick. Arriving at the airport we were quite excited but had doubts as well wondering what lay ahead of us for the next three years in a strange place.

Unfortunately our flight was delayed until late in the evening and we didn't leave until 8.30 p.m.

Our flight from Gatwick was in a Dakota and was quite bumpy which upset some of the passengers. So we were glad when we touched down at Gibraltar airport.

The sight when we landed was quite magnificent. There in a clear sky and framed against the 'Rock' was a huge moon lighting up the area around us.

We were met by the family of a work colleague of mine, Bill Kingford. Bill and his family lived in Ministry of Defence accommodation near the dockyard.

They put us up for several days while we looked for a furnished flat. Next day while looking for a flat we found the temperature was very hot, being well over 100°F. It was the hottest month of August they had for years. Our daughter Louise was streaming with sweat as she was running around similar to what she had done in Newcastle.

After a few days Margaret and I found a flat close to the town centre. Unfortunately we had to climb four flights of stairs to reach the flat, not ideal in the hot weather. So you can guess when we climbed up to the flat in the evening we didn't venture out again until the next day.

During the weekend we had a look around the shops on Main Street. Some of the Indian shops were like bazaars with their displays of colourful ornaments and clothing. We ended up going to the NAAFI to stock up for the next week's groceries.

On the Monday morning I went into the dockyard and

after visiting my senior manager was told that I was to take over the management of the Constructive shops in the North Yard.

I found my office at the corner of the Main Machine Shop. It was small but adequate for my needs. I met the shops staff during the morning.

I found out that nearly all the Inspectors and chargemen were from Britain. I was now one of the 'Raj' that managed the various machine shops and other units in the dockyard.

I noticed another anomaly when I went into the main constructive machine shop at lunchtime; all the Spaniards were sitting on one side and the Gibraltarian workers on the other side of the shop. It seemed 'neither the twain shall meet' although they must have in some cases worked together when undertaking large structure builds for a number of warships undergoing refit in the Yard.

After enquiring about this anomaly I was told the Gibraltarian workers felt they were a cut above the Spanish workers. After further enquiry about the various workmen I found that even the rates of pay were different. The UK craftsmen received the highest rate, the next level of pay was received by the Gibraltarians and the Spanish craftsmen had the lowest rate of pay. I was surprised at the differences as I found out later that some of the most skilled of the craftsmen were the Spanish workmen.

Towards the end of the week, after settling in to my job, I decided to walk across to the offices of the chargeman who looked after the craftsmen working on the ships in refit.

My main reason for the visit was that I would be dealing with them about their many requests for structural items to be manufactured in the Machine Shops.

Another reason for my visit was to be reacquainted with several chargemen who had been in the same year of apprenticeship or worked with me either in Devonport or Rosyth Dockyards.

After chatting with the chargemen I knew, I started to make my way out of the building. As I reached the last office I noticed the door was open. On looking into the office I noticed a chargeman I didn't know with a number of workmen. I couldn't help but notice he was selling bottles of brandy to them.

Around the office on shelves were stacked dozens of bottles of brandy. The place looked like a bootleggers' den. I was told afterwards that some of the Spanish workmen smuggle bottles of brandy across the border for this chargeman so that he could sell the brandy at a cheap price. Later when the senior manager visited the offices of the chargeman all the illicit bottles of brandy had been locked away in cupboards.

During the next few weeks I was busy dealing with the priority of orders for my shops. The blacksmiths' shop was particularly busy with the arrival in the dockyard of the aircraft carrier HMS *Centaur*.

The ship required the changing and testing of chain cable and anchor arrangements. This meant that all the personnel of the Blacksmith Shop and myself would be working overtime including weekends to complete the work on schedule for HMS *Centaur* in order to allow the ship to meet her deadline for recommencing her operational timetable.

During this period my wife Margaret took Louise to Rosia Bay and joined the dockyard Swimming Club.

On Margaret's first visit to Rosia Bay she had her initial

experience of the class distinction operating in the Naval Base. When she walked down the steps that gave access to Rosia Bay she noticed there were two separate flat concrete areas for swimmers. At the bottom of the steps she wondered which area she could go to for swimming. A lady whom she recognised as being from the dockyard Officers accommodation told her she had to go to the right-hand side. The left-hand side was only for Naval Officers and their families.

Here was her introduction to the 'Raj' system adopted on the 'Rock' by the Naval Base Hierarchy.

Although my rank as an Inspector of Trades was equivalent to a Lieutenant in the Royal Navy I was not allowed on the Naval side as I was not on the Naval List.

Despite this rebuff my wife enjoyed the company of the people on the dockyard side. With our daughter Louise they enjoyed many afternoons picnicking or sunbathing at Rosia Bay.

After three weeks of day work and overtime the Blacksmith Shop completed the chain and cable repair and testing for HMS *Centaur*. This allowed the ship staff to make the aircraft carrier ready for sea.

Knowing she was leaving the next day some of my staff and myself went to the berth where the aircraft carrier was moored. Shortly after our arrival at the berthside the dockyard riggers let go of the steel hawsers holding the ship.

With steam up the ship slowly moved away from the berth. Soon it was making its way out of the dockyard. Finally we could only see the outline of her and the slipstream she had left behind.

I felt proud that the staff and I had achieved the work so

that HMS *Centaur*, such a huge ship, could operate again and continue her duties in the Far East.

During the next week our Morris Traveller that we purchased in Newcastle arrived in the Port on a Fleet Auxiliary Ship. After clearing the car's documents at the Customs Office I took Margaret and our daughter Louise for a trip around the Rock.

At the weekend Margaret made up a picnic and we went in the car to the upper reaches of the Rock to see the pack of apes that lived there.

We parked the car and sat on the wall at the upper reaches near to where a number of the apes were sitting on nearby rocks eating fruit. The apes seemed quite harmless but we were warned that they could turn on people and bite them.

A tourist who was nearer to the apes than us came too close to one of the apes and it jumped on his back. It took all the efforts of his two companions to release the ape from his back. There was a lesson to be learnt by the tourist. The ape ran off screaming and chattering until it stopped high up on a ledge just below the top of the Rock.

After the excitement with the apes we had our picnic and I drove back to our flat.

On return to my work on the Monday morning I was told by some of my colleagues that a trip to Tangier had been organised by the dockyard Social Club. They asked me if I was interested in the trip.

That evening I asked my wife if she was interested in the trip. At first Margaret thought the trip was too much for our daughter Louise. After some discussion we felt that Louise was robust enough to withstand the trip across to Morocco. Next day I put our names down for the trip.

On the Saturday we rose early and packed some items for the trip and I drove the three of us in the Morris Traveller to the Port area and parked the car. It was only a short walk to the ship *Mons Calpe* that would take us across to Tangier.

The trip across the straits in the passenger ship was uneventful. Many of the group were quite excited as it was their first trip to Africa.

Once the dockyard group had climbed down the gangway they were gathered together by the chosen leader. A guide was hired to take us around the area.

First he took us to an area just outside Tangier where a number of the party were shown how to ride camels. Some of the group were quite successful with their rides but others kept falling off the camels. Several of the riders had sore bottoms the next day.

Next the guide took us on a visit to the Casbah, the Arabic quarter of Tangier. We all enjoyed the experience and bought items varying from trinkets to camel stools.

Despite the glamour of the Arabic quarter one had a sinister feeling about the quarter with its narrow streets and dark alcoves.

On our way down one of the many rows of steps we had a shock. Close to one of the lower steps there were high walls with recesses. In several of these recesses stood local Arabs in their robes standing still just looking at us.

They looked quite frightening with their gaunt faces, black beards and hooked noses. These men looked at us with their dark piercing eyes. They would have been ideal actors for a horror movie.

The group quickly walked passed them and were glad

when they reached the bottom of the steps and then out of the Casbah.

Although we enjoyed the experience we all said that we didn't want to revisit the Casbah in any future visit to Tangier.

During our walk back from the Casbah two of my colleagues from the dockyard boasted that they had bought a wool blanket for a pound. So out of devilment I was determined to buy a blanket for less than a pound.

A street seller followed me after I offered eighteen shillings, just under a pound, for a blanket. He saw I had the money in silver coins in my hand. We bartered all the way to the ship. Just as I was climbing on board the ship the street seller threw the blanket over my shoulder and took the money I had in my hand. My colleagues were quite disgruntled with my success.

The trip back on the *Mons Calpe* was not so comfortable as a strong wind across the straits caused the ship to roll a lot.

Margaret, Louise and myself were all right but some of the group were sick and were glad when we reached the Port of Gibraltar. On leaving the ship we walked to our car, put our purchases in the back and I drove back to our flat. After eating a snack, as we were not very hungry, we went to our beds early. We had been quite exhilarated with the experience of the trip to Tangier and especially the visit to the Casbah.

A few days later we were told that there was a furnished flat for rent at 23 Cumberland Road. Margaret and I went to look at the flat and although small (the bath you could only sit in to wash), it would be more suitable for us. The flat was close to Rosia Bay for swimming and I could walk to the dockyard for my work.

After we gave Mr Levy our landlord notice of leaving his flat we started to pack our belongings, not that there were many of them.

We moved to the new flat a few days later and settled in. It was a joy not to have to climb up all those flights of stairs in the hot weather to the flat we had now vacated in Cornwall's Parade.

The day after we settled in the flat being a Saturday we drove off in the car to Rosia Bay. We took in turns to go for a swim as Louise was too young to leave on her own. The water was warm and pleasant to swim in. It was my first swim for three years as I didn't go to the local baths in either Dunfermline or Newcastle while we lived there.

For the next week I was busy at work with organising the production of last-minute items in the machine shops for HMS *Cavendish's* refit. It meant the shops working overtime to complete the items and have them fitted prior to the commissioning of the ship.

On 17th September Margaret and I attended the commissioning ceremony. The ship looked like new with all her superstructure painted and new fittings shining in the sun.

Those invited were restricted to Dockyard and Naval Officers involved with the refit and a selection of personnel that were on the Navy List. Again this was the influence of the 'Raj', the higher officials.

With the completion of *Cavendish's* refit I had a free weekend from work. Margaret and I decided to visit Camp Bay instead of Rosia Bay for a swim.

We prepared sandwiches and drinks and went in our car to the parking area near the Bay. To get to the Bay we had to walk through a tunnel cut in the rockface. While walking through the tunnel we had quite a fright.

Margaret who was pushing our daughter Louise in her pram just ahead of me saw something move above her in the tunnel. All of a sudden out of the darkness a snake dropped down, just missing the pram. Luckily the snake moved off quickly away from us.

Despite the scare we enjoyed our picnic at Camp Bay and stayed there most of the day. We came back to our flat in the evening quite content with our day out.

As we were now settled in Gibraltar we had thoughts about going across the border to Spain and a trip up to Estapona which was not too far from Gibraltar.

I was at first reluctant to risk going across the border as my colleagues at work gave a bad impression of Southern Spain. They said the roads were very bad with huge pot holes. Joking, they said you could lose a mini car in one of the holes. You also needed a special insurance and a tow rope in case you had an accident with the bad roads. If the Gardia, the Spanish police, picked you up after an accident you could be thrown into jail and be left without food and water.

Despite these comments we decided we would go, after arranging insurance and visas to get into Spain as well as purchasing a tow rope. We would be adventurous and plan an excursion for a later date.

For our first trip I drove across to La Linea the border town and parked the car in the town square.

At a nearby bar we sat outside and had some sandwiches and soft drinks. Afterwards we had a look around La Linea and saw the bullring with all the placards on the walls advertising future bullfights. Later Margaret found the hairdresser she had been told about. She said that she would arrange with some of the dockyard workers' wives, as she now had a visa, to go across to La Linea and get her hair permed. As well as being able to enjoy the trip the hairdressing costs were cheaper than the hairdressers in Gibraltar.

As we had both played tennis in Newcastle we made enquiries and found there was a dockyard tennis club that played at Queens Way close to the dockyard. We saw the secretary of the club and joined.

We turned up to play the next weekend and found out that most of the players were Inspectors in the dockyard although the club was open to anyone working in the dockyard. Although the weather was hot we enjoyed the tennis and the companionship we struck up with the players.

After two months in charge of the construction shops there was a vacancy that occurred for an Inspector of Shipwrights in the ship refitting section as one of the Inspectors was returning to the UK after completing his three-year tour.

The reason I applied for the job was to obtain experience in ship-refitting work. Fortunately I was given the post and started work right away and moved to the main Inspector of Shipwrights ship refit office. Little did I know of the enormity of the job I had taken on. This would occur about a week later as an urgent ship repair requirement came along.

A tanker called the *Pole Star* had hit a rock near Gibraltar and had major damage to the lower part of her stem.

Details of her docking requirements were provided by the Drawing Office quickly. With these details the dock bottom was prepared with dock blocks to suit the support of the tanker while in dock. Once the tanker was taken into the dock the water was pumped out so that the damaged stern could be examined.

After examination it was decided what part of the stem had to be cut away, so soon after the burners and iron caulkers got to work clearing the damaged metal.

When this was completed shipwrights erected timbers to make a mould to represent the shape of the part of the stem that had been cut out. Some of the timbers used were twenty foot long. The wood mould was taken to the Machine Shop for the part of the stem to be fabricated.

While this work was underway the iron caulkers set to work preparing the remaining part of the stern for welding the prefabricated part in place.

As the tanker was delayed making her destination, the iron caulkers preparing for the weldment from the Machine Shop had to work all day and night. The noise and vibration their work caused disturbed the dockyard families living in the nearby Tower Buildings close to the dock. The families complained to the Senior Management of the dockyard, but were told of the urgency needed so that the tanker could make her scheduled date at her destination.

When the fabricated part of the stem was completed it was put on a low loader truck and transported to the dock.

There the part was lowered into place by a dockside crane and fitted at the lower position at the stem. Next a team of welders set to work to weld the part to the existing stem.

By the evening the fabricated part was completely welded. Next morning the dock was flooded and the tanker moved out.

The management were relieved to see the tanker leave the dock after the completion of a difficult structural repair involving several teams of shipwrights, drillers, welders and iron caulkers to maintain the continuous twenty-four hour working over the repair period.

The relief was short-lived: as the tanker was moving to the South Arm ready to depart, it hit a large fender. The collision caused one of the ship's side plates just above the waterline to be damaged.

The shipwrights quickly found a suitable steel plate in the plate racks nearby and transported it to the South Arm adjacent to the tanker. The damaged ship's side plate was cut out by the burners and the new plate fitted.

The securing of the new steel plate was not straightforward as the edges of the plate had to be welded, but the lower end had to be riveted to match the existing structure.

Again shipwrights, caulkers and welders were working through the day and night to secure the new steel plate. In addition the bottom had to be drilled and riveted using rivets heated in a coke fire and secured by using a power hammer and steel dolly for back up.

As I was in charge of the structural repairs I had to be at the site all day and into the small hours of the next morning. At last by mid-morning the tanker repair was complete and it left for its destination.

Exhausted I went back to our flat and had something to eat. Then I went to bed and slept all the rest of the day and night.

I was hoping I would not have to undertake another urgent task like that one for a long time.

★

Work in the dockyard quietened down so I was able to enjoy not having to work overtime in the evenings or weekends.

Some of my colleagues in the office suggested we visit La Linea and go to the bullring there and watch a bullfight. I knew bullfighting was extremely popular with the Spanish inhabitants in Southern Spain. I was told the bullfight would be spectacular with plenty of colour with flags and streamers and La Linea residents in their colourful finery going to the bullring.

Margaret and I were hesitant about going to the bullfight knowing that the bulls get pierced by the picadors and then killed by the matadors.

After more persuasion we agreed to go; before condemning it I felt that I had to see one bullfight.

On the evening of the event Margaret and I went across with the office group to see the spectacle. Once settled in our seats we could see all the Spanish locals in colourful dresses and suits. The whole bullring was dressed in colourful flags and streamers.

With each bullfight there was plenty of noise and shouting from the crowd at the matadors who were dressed in their glittering outfits, and treated like film stars.

The first couple of bullfights went reasonably well with the matadors making clean kills. The third one was messy with the matador unable to make a clean kill and the scene became quite gory with the bull being speared to weaken it as it was still strong and charging the matador relentlessly. The spearing and the work of the picadors caused the blood to gush from many of the bull's wounds.

In the end the bull was so weakened that the matador was able to easily kill it.

When finally we left the bullring with my colleagues I said seeing the gory sight of the wounded bull before it was killed put me off going to bullfights. We said that we would never go to another bullfight and we never did in the three years we were in Gibraltar.

Although we hadn't lived in our small flat for long we felt that we would like to move to a larger residence. This was especially because we were hoping Margaret's mum and dad would travel from Glasgow and stay with us for a few weeks' holiday. Besides, the flat had not been built correctly and lacked proper ventilation so that green mould was growing on the walls. The only decent window overlooked a broken-down garage. This was not good for our daughter who was only two years old or for me who suffered from asthma sometimes.

After only being in the small flat for three months we were offered a much larger house at Morish Castle. It was an ex-army officer's residence last occupied by a major stationed in Gibraltar.

★

We travelled in the car to the house in Morish Castle as it was a good distance from the flat. When we looked around the house we were quite pleased with it as it had two large and one small bedroom, a lounge and a large kitchen. There was a large garden at the back of the house. In addition the whole house was well furnished ready to walk into at short notice. The only disadvantage was that the house was high up on the Rock and reached by travelling up a very long hill. The only other way to the town centre was by climbing down one hundred steps to Casemates below. The steps were named Jacobs Ladder.

So again we packed our belongings which were not very bulky other than a playpen for our daughter Louise. As the house was furnished we settled into it quite easily. At the weekend we stocked up with groceries so as not to have to buy much during the week.

While I was working in the dockyard, Margaret with Louise took the bus down the long hill to the town centre. Halfway down an amazing thing happened. The driver got out of the bus and bought lottery tickets for anyone on the bus who wanted to purchase tickets. Seemingly this was a regular occurrence on this bus route.

Once we had settled in for about a week we decided to have a housewarming party. I invited all the Inspectors and chargemen in the ship refitting group as well as their wives. I got acceptance for about twenty so I thought that I had better do something about catering for the party. As it was quite a large number I made enquiries for someone to cater for that number. I ended up hiring a chef who did catering for the army barracks. I gave him details of the numbers coming and the mixture of food we wanted for that evening.

Having such a large number of guests I realised that I would have to purchase a mixture of drinks such as beers and other alcoholic drinks.

With tongue in cheek I rang a Wine and Spirits Merchant in Gibraltar and said to the manager that I was going to be entertaining quite often during the next three years, I was working for the Ministry of Defence and he readily granted me discounts for any of the produce I purchased from his company. I was pleasantly surprised to get the discount agreement as I am sure I would not have obtained an agreement like that in Britain.

The army chef who had the rank of corporal came to our house and saw the layout of the kitchen and told us what he would prepare for the party. It was agreed that we would pay him ten (old) shillings per head which was a surprisingly cheap deal for the food he would provide.

On the afternoon before the party evening the chef brought all the food and laid it out in the kitchen. I was amazed how much food he brought along. There was cooked chicken, cold meats, pies and a variety of sweets.

The party started well with drinks and a chat. Then the chef laid out the food on tables and the visitors tucked into the chicken and cold meats as well as pies and other delicacies. This was followed with guests choosing from the variety of sweets.

Afterwards we played games such as musical chairs and the dancers standing on the folding newspaper game. It became fast and furious as each time when a couple didn't keep still on a newspaper when the music was stopped they were eliminated and the competitors left had time to fold their newspaper before the music started again. As the game progressed the couples found it harder and harder as each time the music stopped a couple was eliminated who were unable to stand still on the many times folded newspaper. It ended up with the remaining lady being lifted off the floor because the folded paper was so tiny.

After the games the visitors went out into the garden to see the view over the bay to the airport below and Spain beyond. The air was quite balmy so it was quite enjoyable chatting in the garden.

Afterwards we all went into the house and one of the guests, a chargeman who came from Scotland, had a good singing voice and sang a number of Scottish songs. Finally the guests left, quite contented, and drove off in their cars back to their own flats.

Even though the guests had eaten quite well we had a large amount of food left over that would last us for weeks.

Later in the month we heard that the army chef we hired for the party was brought up for court martial for stealing provisions from the army stores.

I told my boss about the situation and he said to forget all about it. "You didn't know if he stole food for your party," but the circumstances of the cheap price paid for the food made the circumstances suspicious.

★

Some of the evenings when we were sitting on the roof and the sky was clear we could see police launches in the Bay chasing unmarked boats trying to bring contraband into Gibraltar.

The well-known Victory brothers in their large launch were chased by the police quite often with shots being fired. We could see searchlights panning the water between Gibraltar and Spain. It was better than seeing a crime movie – being the real thing.

★

As we were now settled in Gibraltar and had already gone across the border to La Linea we decided to go further afield.

One weekend as planned we decided to visit Estapona which was only a short distance along the Spanish coast from Gibraltar. Although the roads were bad with plenty of potholes we made good time as there was little traffic on the road.

We stayed in the only hotel in Estapona and found the hotel was excellent with clean airy rooms and the food, although Spanish cuisine, quite good. We found after the first day at the hotel that the Malaga football team had stayed there. It was surprising as Estapona in the 1960s was just a sleepy small fishing village.

Next morning we had a continental breakfast in the hotel; you couldn't get a fried breakfast but you could ask for an omelette as an extra. As the weather was fine we drove to Torremolinos that was not far from Estapona. I was told it was becoming popular for American visitors. Torremolinos was much bigger than Estapona with fine buildings and a beautiful square. After looking around the town centre we stopped at a roadside café where we had some sandwiches and soft drinks. I found the Spanish coffee too strong for me.

We returned to the hotel in late afternoon and after resting because the weather was hot we dressed for dinner. Although the dinner was Spanish style, it was well cooked and we enjoyed it. The local wine was weak, but we enjoyed it.

Next day we just sat in the hotel garden and enjoyed the sunshine but we were all well oiled up, especially our daughter who had a fair skin.

Many of the hotel staff would walk past Louise and touch her hair and say "rubio"(red). It seems to be an unusual colour of hair in Spain. They said touching it would give them good luck.

On the Sunday we returned to our house in Gibraltar quite content with the weekend holiday.

★

On return to work I found that a contract had been placed by Rand Shipping Company for the dockyard to undertake the survey of the *Mons Calpe* ship's hull and to renew any rusted steel plating, also clean down and repaint the whole of the hull. In addition some wood decking repairs had to be carried out. The Rand Shipping Company had hired another passenger ferry to undertake the daily crossing from Gibraltar to Tangier.

As the *Mons Calpe* was a small ship the dockyard management decided to place a spare dock caisson in the dock to undertake a hull survey and have it cleaned down and repainted. As it was a small ship I was given the task of looking after the work on the ship and dock caisson.

The dock was prepared with dock blocks to take the ship and the dock caisson. This was completed in quite a short time as only a small number of dock blocks were required for the two vessels.

First the caisson was brought into the flooded dock and then the *Mons Calpe*. During the docking down of the two vessels the weather started to turn and we experienced a heavy wind that started to move the caisson, which was tall and wall sided, across the dock. I immediately shouted to the chargeman of shipwrights to attach two extra wires tying the caisson to the centre of the dock. With the extra wires we were able to bring the caisson back over the blocks position.

From then on the docking was straightforward. When

the dock pumping-out stopped at about two or three feet above the blocks the diver went down to check that the landing on the blocks were clear of any debris.

Once the diver had completed his examination and the blocks were clear the pumping out started again. Quite a number of the local workmen jumped into the water and started to catch fish. Some of the workmen were successful and got some good-sized fish. Other workmen not so experienced were floundering around in the water with the fish too slippery for them.

The workmen, chargemen and myself watching the men floundering could not help laughing at their antics.

I was told afterwards that when any ship was docked down it was a ritual for workmen to jump in the water and try and catch fish, so that night some of the locals had fish suppers.

The work on the *Mons Calpe* went reasonably well, but I had to battle with the Inspectors working on the Destroyer *Carysford* (which was undergoing a long refit from November 1962 to May 1964), for the transfer of welders and iron caulkers to the *Mons Calpe* repair as quite a number of shipside plates were badly rusted and had to be replaced.

Despite the additional shipside plate-work the ship was finished on time and handed back to the Rand Shipping Company.

The following weekend I took Margaret and daughter Louise down to the Port where the *Mons Calpe* was berthed in readiness for her voyage across to Tangier.

The ship looked splendid with the shipsides and superstructure new paintwork shining in the sun and the new wooden deck making it look like a new ship. Any of the workmen who were employed on the project would be proud to see the ship in pristine condition.

★

During the next week the North Yard where I worked was reasonably quiet. The workmen were clearing up the dockside and putting wood shores that had been used for the *Mons Calpe* docking into storage areas.

During that week the Foreman of the Yard, my boss, Bill Lock said to me, "Rest while you can as I think there is a big job coming to Gibraltar. It could be bigger than the tanker repair." He would not tell me what the project was and just smiled as he walked off with plans under his arm heading for the drawing office.

At the time I didn't believe him as the tanker repair was a difficult job. Little did I know how enormous the job would be to take on for a small dockyard.

After a few days the Foreman of Yard called all the Inspectors into his office and said we had been given the project of undertaking large-scale repairs and the fitting of the ski lift alteration on the flight deck of HMS *Ark Royal*. She was 42,000 tons, the biggest ship in the Royal Navy. Gibraltar Dockyard had never undertaken a task of this magnitude.

All the Inspectors at first were speechless, understanding the enormity of the task.

Each Inspector was given a work package for their respective specialisation. There was one for the electrical section, another for the mechanical section. I was given the one for the constructive section. We had to take the work packages away and study their content for planning the work. On return each Inspector had to say what manpower and materials were needed. In some cases specialised items had already been detailed in the work packages and these would be delivered in the next week.

Because of the size of the constructive package I told the Foreman of the Yard that I would need to have shipwrights transferred from the Southern Yard.

Our first task was to dock this enormous ship in our largest dock, the No 1 Dock. I obtained the docking plan from the drawing office. The size of the blocks and wooden shores needed for the docking was huge. It took several days to set out the dock blocks and prepare the wooden shores.

With the arrival of the *Ark Royal* at the Port in Gibraltar there were many spectators at the Port to see the massive ship move in.

Then the tugs took over so that she was moved to the South Arm opposite the dockyard. At the South Arm munitions and some toxic materials were removed. The Customs Officers went aboard and checked through the ship for contraband. This done the tugs started to move the ship towards the flooded No 1 Dock with the outer caisson removed.

By this time strong winds had sprung up and the tugs had difficulty getting the ship to enter the flooded dock in a central position. The dockyard workers transferred heavy wire hawsers to the ship and the shore ends connected to electric driven capstans each side of the dock, two at the entry end and two at the closed caisson end of the dock.

Gradually, by operating the capstans, the hawser wires were drawn in slowly moving the ship centrally into the dock.

By this time the wind was becoming much stronger and its force was trying to push the ship to the side of the dock.

I was watching the wires at the entrance end and my boss Bill Lock, the Foreman of the Yard and experienced in the docking of large ships at Devonport and Singapore Dockyards, at the fixed caisson end.

With a sudden gust of stronger wind a wire snapped with the loose end just missing one of the workmen on the capstan. Bill Lock rushed along the dock and said in a loud voice to me, "I will take over." So another wire was quickly put over to the ship to hold it and then the wire on the other side snapped.

Bill Lock snorted when this happened and said to me, "I will leave you to it," and went back to the position of the tied wires at the fixed caisson end. I shouted for another wire to be transferred to the ship and secured. By this time the ship had entered into the dock and the dock sides and nearside building gave some protection from the wind.

As soon as the ship was in the dock the caisson was quickly closed and the water was being pumped out.

We sighed with relief once we knew the ship was safely held in the dock. If a second wire had snapped before we replaced the broken one the *Ark Royal* could have crashed into the dock wall causing considerable damage.

As standard practice the pumping out of the water was stopped with the water level just above the top of the docking blocks. Then the diver went down and checked that the top of the blocks was clear of debris.

Once the diver had come up the pumping out started again and, as in previous dockings, some of the workmen jumped into the water to catch any fish that had been trapped when the caisson was closed.

This time the workmen didn't find it very easy to catch the fish and were floundering around in the water as the fish were much larger and their skins very slippery.

As the water was pumped down lower we could see there were hundreds of fish in the water and some of them were very large. Once the water was nearly drained out the workmen managed to catch some of the smaller fish.

Finally when the dock was nearly dry we could see a massive number of tuna, a large dark fish. As one of the old workmen said it must have been a shoal of tuna that followed in behind the ship looking for food. When the dock was dry workmen were carrying away loads of the tuna fish.

The amount of fish was so massive we were ringing up the hospitals and other organisations asking them to take considerable amounts of fish.

I managed to take home a large tuna and put it in the fridge. Our Constructive Manager contacted me and said he didn't have any fish so I had to cut my fish which was quite large and arrange for one of the workmen to take half of my fish to his house.

With so much fish taken out of the dockyard I think most homes would have fish suppers that night.

Despite so much fish being taken out of the dockyard I found that there was so much fish left that I was worried that the fish would quickly rot and smell, therefore becoming a health risk. On the Friday I went to see my boss Bill Lock and asked him for permission to bring in a squad on overtime for the Saturday and Sunday and shovel the rotting fish into skips. He agreed especially as he was told that it was estimated that seventy tons of fish had come into the dock with the *Ark Royal*. It took the full two days to shovel the fish into the skips so that they could be dumped at sea!

For many weeks after this many households had tuna steaks for their dinners.

★

To start the constructive work on the *Ark Royal* I set up two gangs of shipwrights. The shipwrights with their chargeman from the South Yard to undertake internal work on extensive accommodation repairs, including messes and bathrooms. The North Yard chargeman and his gang of shipwrights to undertake the outer bottom work and the ski lift modification on the flight deck. The first task on the ship was cleaning off marine growth and vegetation from the outer bottom of the ship by the painters section. This to be followed by the coating of the outer bottom with anti-fouling paints. For the shipwrights most of the protective zincs needed to be renewed especially those in way of non-ferrous fittings such as the propeller, rudder shaft sleeves and hull valves where there was the most galvanic action to the plating of the outer bottom.

Work on the ski lift took place early with the clearance of some fittings on the flight deck before the fabrication of the ski lift modification to the flight deck took place.

All the work on the ship went well although the ski lift work was the most difficult needing long hours of work with shipwrights and welders sometimes working from six in the morning until late in the evenings.

★

There were three interesting incidents that took place during the ships repair period. Two of the incidents were amusing but the third one was not amusing at all.

The first incident took place during the ship repair period when an old shipwright often lost his way when trying to get to his workplace in a mess in one of the lower decks and out again. He solved the problem by marking his route to the mess with chalk marks – quite ingenious.

The second incident was when one of the workmen took two duffle coats that were left in a mess. He decided to get them out of the dockyard by wearing them below his own top coat. With all three coats on he looked like a fat teddy bear. He was soon caught by the police as he tried to go out through the main dockyard gate!

The final incident was not very amusing. On one of the Saturdays during the ship's repair period I had forgotten to examine a completed repair in one of the small compartments low down in the ship, so I decided to go on my own to examine the repair. To get to it I had to climb down through a manhole with a bar across it. With an effort I managed to squeeze through the manhole into the compartment.

After scrambling around the compartment checking the repair I started to get hot in my overalls. So, satisfied with the repair, I tried to get through the manhole and got stuck because my body had swelled with the exertion in the compartment. As the compartment was in a remote part of the ship I could not shout for help if I couldn't get out.

Deciding not to panic I dropped back into the compartment and took off my overalls and sat down and waited until I cooled down. Then when I had cooled down I threw my overalls out through the manhole and managed to squeeze through. It taught me a lesson as next time when there was similar work to inspect I would have another person standing by to avoid a possible accident.

The ship's repair and ski lift project was completed on time. It was a very condensed period, starting on Friday the 22nd March 1963 and completing with its undocking on Monday the 22nd April 1963.

Bill Lock the Foreman of the Yard called to his office all the Inspectors of the main specialisations and thanked them for their efforts with a small workforce during a very limited period.

Near the end of the ship's repair period when I was looking at the final completion work taking place on the ski lift modifications I was approached by two Naval lieutenants involved with the project.

As I climbed down from the structure one of the officers just casually said, "I presume you are attending the cocktail party tonight." He was surprised when I told him that I had not been invited to it as I was not on the Navy List (the Gibraltar Raj in action again).

The officer said he could not believe it as he said, "You have worked long hours on this repair project."

Instantly both Naval officers said to me, "You go back home and tell your wife to get dressed and come along to the gangway at seven o'clock and we will be waiting for you. Just wait there for a few minutes and I will get you two tickets for the party."

As soon as I could get away I drove home and told my wife Margaret what had happened. Luckily we managed to get Anne Fisher, a daughter of one of the Mechanical Inspectors, to babysit for us.

So about ten to seven that evening we were all dressed up and I drove us to the ship in our Minor Traveller.

On parking the car we walked to the ship's gangway. Not only were the two young Naval officers waiting for us but a whole group of young Naval lieutenants and midshipmen too. They had been told about the attitude of the decision makers using the Navy List for invitations.

On the huge hanger deck there was a large crowd and with the young Naval officers we had a great time. It was one of the best evenings we had ever spent in Gibraltar thanks to the young Naval officers going against protocol.

★

In the next week I offered to take Roy Hare, an Inspector of Shipwrights in the dockyard, to pick up his wife at the airport.

Before we came to Gibraltar Roy and I had both worked in Newcastle, but in different areas. Roy and Margaret Hare visited us in Newcastle before we left for Gibraltar.

So I took Margaret, Louise and Roy to the airport and picked up Roy's wife. From the airport I took Roy, Margaret and Louise to the furnished flat Roy had rented in the centre of the town. When we went into the flat the two Margarets and I were amazed at the poor condition of the flat. It was small and dark with only one decent window. In the bedroom which was quite old, the beds were broken and the bed legs were tied together with rope.

Margaret and I didn't say anything but afterwards I said that Roy who always counted his pennies had paid a moderate price for an inadequate flat for Margaret and himself after leaving an excellent house in a select part of

Newcastle to come to Gibraltar. It must be said the local businessmen overcharged for flats because of the shortage in Gibraltar.

Later I heard from Roy that his wife had said she was very unhappy with such a horrible flat and threatened to go back on the next flight to Britain.

Roy managed to appease her and after about a week he managed to get a much better furnished flat, although much more expensive, near the Parade Square in town.

The problem with trying to hire accommodation was because there was not enough Ministry of Defence accommodation for all the UK workers and staff. In most cases a member of staff or workman had to wait some time until a UK worker or staff member left Gibraltar at the end of their tour. Then that flat was handed over to the next person on the waiting list.

We were lucky with the house at Morish Castle as we were able to rent it from the army organisation at a reasonable cost.

It was not long after the Hares moved to the better flat that, being on the top of the MOD waiting list, we got a move to the Old Naval Hospital grounds. The house was on top of a slope which gave us a good view over the dockyard and port.

It was a three-bedroom furnished house with excellent facilities for our family. It was much handier as I could walk to the dockyard and there were some small shops nearby. This large house gave Margaret the chance to invite her parents in Glasgow out to Gibraltar for a long holiday.

During the next week I had an attack of asthma so I went to the doctor in the dockyard, who was a Naval officer.

When he examined me he found that my lungs were quite congested. Not being very expert on this type of illness he played safe and sent me to the Naval Hospital. At the hospital I was examined by the Consultant who prescribed antibiotics and some medicine I didn't know about a new drug called prednisolone. The antibiotics started to clear my congested lungs and the prednisolone started to reduce my asthma attack.

Within two days the large dosages of prednisolone reduced the asthma attack considerably. The one drawback with such high dosages of the drug is that I had insomnia and didn't sleep very much those nights. When the drug was reduced I slept like a log.

By the end of the week I was feeling much better. Margaret who came to see me every day as she managed to get a babysitter, had to travel by bus each time.

The next day I was sent home but had to stay off my work for a bit longer. On returning home Margaret said she wanted to learn to drive the car especially as our car was unused all the time I was in the hospital.

After making several inquiries Margaret managed to get a local lady who was a Driving instructor and right away had her first lesson. She found that most of the streets were very narrow and the local drivers drove very fast, but she managed to cope at her lesson. The driving inspector told her that in later lessons she would have to learn how to reverse and park in a small space as it is one of the parts of the driving test she would have to pass.

★

As I was still off my work I suggested to Margaret that we

take a trip to Ronda as I had been told that it was a place worth seeing because it was so picturesque. Margaret agreed as it would be a change to get away from Gibraltar.

I was told how difficult the journey would be with the car on the road to Ronda. Despite this I booked a hotel in Ronda and we set off the next morning with sufficient clothes to last us for several days.

Leaving Gibraltar I drove the Morris Traveller along the Spanish coast for quite a distance but had no trouble as there wasn't much traffic, although the condition of the road was poor with plenty of potholes.

Now the fun started, as beyond the turning off near Torremolinos we were on a road that had a steep climb and the road became quite narrow. Although the road was narrow several vans rushed past us going down the steep hill. Each time this happened it caused me to slow down as I thought a van would clip the car's wing mirror or scrape the side of the car. This was especially so on the tight bends.

Higher up we could see looking out of the car window there was a sheer drop from the outer edge of the road. In some places it was over a hundred feet!

I was glad when we reached Ronda and found the Reina Christina, the hotel we had booked into for our stay. It was a delightful old Spanish style hotel with a beautifully laid out garden. The receptionist who spoke good English with a Spanish accent showed us to our room and told us what we could have for our dinner.

The bedroom was large and airy with large windows. The furniture was Spanish but of a good quality. The hotel also provided a small bed for Louise.

After settling in we had a walk around the back garden

that faced on to the valley. It was long and narrow with a scattering of small shrubs in flower. Placed all along the garden were huge earthenware jars with their open ends to the air. You could imagine they had come from Aladdin's Cave in the Arabian Nights story. We had an excellent dinner and went to bed early. Earlier we had checked that Louise was safe in her little bed. We were all tired after quite an eventful day with the car journey on the mountain road.

After a good night's sleep I woke up and walked to the window. Looking out all I could see was the valley completely covered in mist. It seemed quite eerie, one could imagine oneself in heaven. I woke up Margaret and told her what I saw and she approached the window and after looking out was amazed to see the mist filling the valley.

As we were hungry I ordered breakfast which would normally be a continental breakfast, but I asked for hard-boiled eggs to be added to the breakfast saying I wanted them boiled for six minutes. When the breakfast was delivered we enjoyed the coffee and toast with butter and jam. The only disappointment was that the boiled eggs were soft and watery and not hard.

After breakfast we got well wrapped up as Ronda, being high up, was cool in the morning. We walked around the town and admired the old buildings with their red pantile roofs and white walls. The town was picturesque and seemed to have stood still for hundreds of years.

Then we made our way to the Bullring. Luckily there was a guide at the entrance who showed us around the Bullring. He told us that this was the oldest Bullring in the world. He took us into the Bullring museum where he described the dress of previous matadors, picadors and other officials hanging on the walls.

When we came out of the Bullring Margaret saw an old lady in a black dress sitting on a chair nearby crocheting a table cover with different colour threads. She asked the lady as the table cover was nearly finished if she would sell the cover to her. The lady asked for a sum in pesetas which Margaret paid her and took the table cover, quite pleased to have something to remind her of our Ronda visit.

We were pleased with our visit to the Bullring so went to a local bar and sat outside as it was fine weather and had some drinks and sweet cakes. Louise enjoyed the sweet cakes. We returned to the hotel as Louise would need to rest as she was less than three years old. Later, well rested, we went downstairs to the dining room for dinner. There were several other guests at tables having dinner when we entered the room. Again our meals were well cooked and Margaret and I had some of the local wine.

The next morning I ordered again for our breakfast to be served in our bedroom. To try and get hard-boiled eggs this time I added another minute to the boiling time. Unfortunately the eggs that were delivered were still soft and watery.

After breakfast we walked to the old stone bridge with its huge arches rising up from the valley floor. There we could look down to the valley more than a hundred feet below. While we were there other tourists were present who were taking photographs of the bridge and the valley below.

After a while we went along to the same bar and had served some excellent ham sandwiches with our drinks.

We returned to our hotel quite pleased with our visit

to the town and went to our room where we were glad to rest for a few hours.

Later we went downstairs to the dining room for our meal. The meal was very Spanish but very enjoyable. It was the first time we had a Spanish omelette which was very filling and quite tasty with its mixture of vegetables. Again at breakfast I added another minute for the timing of our boiled eggs but when the waiter came up with coffee, toast and boiled eggs the eggs were still soft and watery. I gave up after that of ever getting a hard-boiled egg at the hotel!

It was late in the morning when we left the hotel and I started to drive down the mountain road. This time I was on the cliff side of the road and just looking out down to the valley below was quite scary.

I tried to keep as far away from the cliff edge as possible as there wasn't any walls or fences to stop a car going over. We still had the Spanish vans tearing past us on the tight bends. Was I glad when we got to the bottom of the mountain road.

The rest of the trip was fairly comfortable from the turning near Torremelinos to Gibraltar.

It was good to get back to our home in Gibraltar but we thoroughly enjoyed the unusual visit to Ronda.

★

In relating previously about trying to get hard-boiled eggs in a hotel in Ronda reminded me of another occurrence relating to hard-boiled eggs.

In Gibraltar on many occasions when a UK worker or staff member is returning to Britain after his three-year tour men of his particular section in the dockyard would take him out for a drink in La Linea a few days before his departure.

There was one occasion in our section of the dockyard when the Welfare Officer Gerry Hill was going back to Britain. So several members of the group, including myself, who wouldn't be drinking volunteered to take our cars across to La Linea on a chosen evening.

Everyone going on the outing were either driving or picked up by cars and taken across the border to La Linea, stopping first to get our visa stamped at the Spanish border.

As usual we made our way to the first tapa bar. There the drinkers had wine or beers. The tapas in the bar were in most cases small pieces of toast and ham. After some drinks we went to other bars for drinks finally stopping at our favourite tapa bar. By this time Gerry Hill had quite a few drinks while I only had drunk tonic water and lemon. On the bar itself there were several jars of hard-boiled eggs.

Gerry, being in a boastful mood said he could drink anyone there in the group under the table!

Most of the group members were hesitant. Although I had not had a drink, for devilment I gave him a challenge that I would eat a hard-boiled egg every time he had a drink. Thinking this would be an easy challenge to win he accepted it.

At first the drinks and boiled eggs went down fast. After six drinks and six eggs we both slowed down. I was starting to feel full but kept on going. When it got to nine eggs Gerry was looking glassy-eyed.

By sheer willpower I reached a total of twelve hard -boiled eggs and Gerry just slid down off the bar stool out for the count.

A couple of the members of the group carried Gerry to their car. I had to hold myself and not be sick – I am sure no one wanted to come near me the next day!

On the way back to the border a number of the group were staggering even though they had eaten tapas at every bar which helped to absorb the alcohol they consumed.

One Inspector of Shipwrights who hadn't drunk very much during the evening took out his keys for his car but slipped and dropped his keys through a drain grating. Luckily the drain was dry and we managed to lift up the grating and retrieve the car keys. Overall we had a great evening out in La Linea. Next day in the dockyard there were plenty of laughs about the hard-boiled eggs versus the drinks challenge. Gerry had to take the kidding on as well as a very sore head. I didn't eat another hard-boiled egg for a very long time.

★

On the Monday morning when I returned to the Inspectors' Office after being declared fit for work by the Naval Doctor, Roy Hare, my colleague who was the Yard Facilities Inspector, was waiting for me. First, he asked me how I was after my recent illness. I replied that I was quite recovered especially after enjoying the clear fresh air of the stay in Ronda.

He said that he had good news. At last he had been allocated a Ministry of Defence house. He added that his wife and himself had looked at the house which was near the entrance gate of the Old Naval Hospital. It was only a short walk down the slope from our house. As he didn't have a car he asked me if I could take their possessions from their flat near the Parade Ground to the chosen house.

I said, "Certainly I will take you." So we fixed that we would take them and their possessions to the house on the following Wednesday. On the Wednesday we collected Roy and Margaret Hare and stowed their possessions in the back of our Morris Traveller and took them to the allocated house.

As the house was furnished it didn't take them long to settle in. Knowing that they hadn't prepared a meal Margaret invited them up to our house for a meal which Margaret had prepared earlier. After the meal we all sat in the lounge and chatted.

It seemed that although they had been in their flat some time they hadn't gone across the border into Spain. I think they were a little apprehensive of risking a trip into Spain. Margaret Hare seemed quite lively; she was in her early thirties and about eight years younger than Roy who seemed set in his ways and was content to make visits to places in Gibraltar.

I said that some time we could take them to Ronda as we felt the place was so spectacular. By the look on Roy's face it would take a lot of persuasion to get him to go there. Apart from his reluctance to go across the Spanish border we did go out together for dinners at some of the hotels and restaurants in Gibraltar.

★

During the week I had returned to work I was called up to the Foreman of Yard's office. There my boss Bill Lock told me that in just over two weeks time we would have to dock the nuclear submarine HMS *Dreadnought* for routine maintenance and checks on the state of the hull.

He told me that I would have to go to the Drawing Office to obtain the docking plan for the submarine. The huge curved docking blocks would arrive next week and be assembled and secured to the dock floor in accordance with the docking plan.

He went on to say that I had to be the dockmaster for the docking as he and his family would be on holiday when the submarine arrived.

When I gave him a queer look as it was a very important docking of a nuclear submarine, he said, "You have successfully completed a number of different ship dockings and I am confident that you will carry out the submarine docking successfully."

So off I went to the Drawing Office and the Senior Draughtsman Peter Vaun explained the set-up of the huge curved blocks to take the hull shape of the submarine in No 3 Dock.

He went on to say that this was the first docking of the nuclear submarine since it left the Camell Lairds building yard on its completion. So quite a first for Gibraltar Dockyard and myself.

Once I had the docking plan I called the chargemen concerned and asked them to come up to the Inspectors' Office and go over the docking arrangements with them. After they had looked at the docking plan they were quite happy with the docking details.

The next week the huge wooden docking blocks with their reinforced steel supports arrived by cargo ship and were transported to No 3 Dock. When I saw them unloaded I was taken aback by the huge size of each dock block and its large curvature to take the shape of the submarine's hull.

With the dock block positions already marked out on the dock floor the set of docking blocks were soon placed and secured. We were now ready to dock HMS *Dreadnought* and No 3 Dock was flooded to a set height for the suitable entry of the submarine.

★

The next week the submarine came in quite silently into the Bay of Gibraltar. It looked a quite fearsome vessel approaching the dockyard. It was soon secured to the tugs with heavy hawser wires. As the tugs moved the submarine to the dock the outer caisson was opened and the submarine entered when wires were transferred to the dockside to be held by the electrical driven capstans.

The submarine went into the dock quite smoothly as it was a calm day. It was then carefully centred over the dock blocks using marked cross wires.

As the water was pumped out of the dock the cross wires were still used to ensure the submarine was still centred over the blocks. When the water was a few feet off the blocks the diver was sent down to check that there was no debris in way of the blocks. In addition he had to check that projections below the hull would not hit any of the blocks when the submarine dropped into the curved form of the wooden blocks.

Once the dock was dry notices were put in place in way of areas of radioactivity. Immediately maintenance work was started on the hull and onboard.

The next day one of the top managers came rushing down to the North Yard and told me that the propeller was on the secret list and had to be covered. The workmen went off and produced several large tarpaulins which were used to cover and tie up the propeller.

Although there were Russian cargo ships in the vicinity it would not be known if they saw the propeller before it was covered!

After a week of routine maintenance where the main work to be done was the changing of some protection zincs against galvanic action on the hull the submarine undocked without any problems and silently went on to its patrol. It was quite a satisfactory period of work with no hiccups.

★

During the next few weeks Margaret had a number of driving lessons from a Gibraltar lady and managed to pass her driving test first time. She now had two driving licences, a Gibraltar one and a UK provisional driving licence.

In one of the conversations with the lady Margaret remarked about learning Spanish. The driving instructor said that her sister who had been a teacher, but was unemployed as she was bringing up a family might be interested in teaching us Spanish. The next week we had a call from her sister who said she would give us some lessons.

So during the next couple of months we had a number of Spanish lessons from her.

As we became friendly with the two sisters we asked them if they would like to go out for dinner one evening which they accepted. At the next weekend I booked dinner for the four of us at a local restaurant in Catalan Bay as suggested by them.

On the Saturday when the four of us arrived at the

restaurant we were serenaded by three men playing mandolins. The music was quite enjoyable.

The head waiter explained that in Catalan Bay there was an Italian colony that had grown up over the years after several Italian families settled there many years ago. The three mandolin players had Italian roots.

The head waiter went on to say that at Christmas time there is a concert in Catalan Bay where several men from the Italian families play a variety of instruments and sing favourite Italian songs.

After the head waiter finished portraying the Catalan Bay history we had our meal which as you can guess was mostly Italian dishes. The four of us decided on Italian dishes and enjoyed them with a suitable Italian wine.

It was quite a change for Margaret and I, but for the Gibraltar ladies it was quite normal as they visited this restaurant quite often.

★

After the dinner one of the sisters suggested that we visit the Casino at the Rock Hotel. As it was a posh hotel, where the actors Sean Connery and Diana Cilento spent their honeymoon, Margaret and I were a bit reluctant but were persuaded to go.

So off we went in two cars to the hotel and parked outside. As the Casino was in the hotel we had to be nosy and see some of the layout of the hotel before entering the Casino. In the Casino there was quite a crowd of people playing the various games. Many of the crowd were of different nationalities.

We made our way to the roulette table where there

weren't too many people playing roulette. We didn't bet very much but all of the ladies won small sums of money. For myself I had a bit of luck as I first won £35 by placing my bet on zero which came up on the spin. I forgot to take the counter off zero and the spin again stopped at zero so I won another £35. Overall I had won over £100 – not a bad sum of money to win in the 1960s.

Overall the evening out with the Gibraltar ladies was a great success. The next weekend I went out and bought a cam recorder with some of my winnings.

We continued with our Spanish lessons as learning basic Spanish would be useful to use on our holidays in Spain. For myself if was useful when speaking to Spanish workers on the job in the dockyard.

★

Shortly after our night out in Catalan Bay I went along to the annual general meeting of the Rosia Swimming Club. For my sins I was appointed the new chairman. Mervyn Gruit who was a shipwright from Devonport and in one of my gangs in the dockyard was made the secretary.

At our first committee meeting we discussed the future prospects at Rosia. I had a good look at the site and all it contained was a long strip of concrete about twenty feet wide next to the water and a small strip of sand when the tide was out adjacent to it. In addition there was a square wooden raft in a bad condition with the paintwork on it falling off tied alongside the strip.

Considering that there were now problems at the Spanish border with hold-ups of cars from time to time and the Spanish Government threatening to close the border we felt that we had to do something to improve the Rosia site for dockyard families using it.

The committee gave me a mandate to work with a UK draughtsman on the committee to draw up a layout of a building and a concrete paddling pool for the young children. After taking some measurements at the site the draughtsman drew out a plan that showed a small kiosk and kitchen, two changing rooms, a store and paddling pool.

When the plan was put before the committee it was given wholehearted approval. The only snag was that the club only had a limited amount of money and would have to scrounge for some materials in the dockyard.

On the committee one of the members was a building manager in the dockyard. He said he would take on the task of clerk of works for the project.

Luckily I had some good connections in the dockyard and started to gather together surplus material including timber that the Naval Stores Section transported to Rosia.

My name started to get known in the dockyard for scrounging materials for use at Rosia. There was one funny incident about this time.

★

We were competing with the Naval Officers Swimming Club who had a similar area to us on the concrete area opposite ours. Their club was building a similar unit to us. As it happened a cargo ship that had berthed in the dockyard and left a pile of planks of timber on the dockside before it sailed.

The Port Admiral heard of this left timber and contacted the Naval Officers Swimming Club committee and knowing of my reputation for scrounging materials said to them to get that timber before Toye gets it. Believe it or not Toye did get there first and the timber was swiftly transferred to our side of Rosia!

The work on the building went well as many of the UK tradesmen could put their hands to most of the building work and soon the shell of the building was created using breeze blocks and timber from the cargo vessel.

It went well until we started to run out of money for materials. One weekend I said to the clerk of works person who was organising the build that we had run out of cement and money!

He just smiled at me and said it's Saturday and it will be quiet in the dockyard today. We will pick up my truck in the dockyard building yard so bring a couple of workers along.

So we went in his car to the yard and picked up the truck. Then he drove us over to the building store where the cement was piled up. We all lent a hand to fill the low-sided truck with bags of cement.

Now we had to get the cement out of the dockyard without being caught by the authorities. Anyway we got to the dockyard gate and unfortunately one of the bags of cement fell off the truck close to where the dockyard police were guarding the gate. My heart was in my mouth as I thought the police would question what we were doing in the yard. The clerk of works calmly went over to the policeman and chatted to him. I couldn't help laughing as the policeman came over and helped me put the bag of cement on the truck. Was I glad when the clerk of works drove the truck out of the gate and then on to Rosia where we unloaded the bags of cement with a sigh of relief.

My immediate boss Bill Lock, Foreman of the Yard, was very pessimistic about our building project at Rosia initially. He even went on to say part-way through the project that if I was lucky enough to get forty persons from the dockyard families to help with the project he would give me a day's work on the site. Little did he know that all the dockyard families were keen on the project and near the end of the building I did get forty persons giving help at Rosia. Unfortunately I still didn't get Bill Lock to give me a day's work. I think he was too embarrassed to turn up.

The help the dockyard families gave us was tremendous, we even had a UK welder welding up all the steel bars to make up the storage racks in the store.

The building was finished off with a corrugated sloping roof and the paddling pool had an awning on top of steel posts to keep the sun off the children in the pool.

The children of the dockyard families played their part. They repaired the wooden raft and repainted it in bright colours. It really looked good anchored in the water opposite the building.

To crown it all we had an opening ceremony with flags and bunting and because he did so much for the project we invited the Clerk of Work's wife to cut the tape at the entrance near the new building.

We all had food and drinks afterwards provided by the wives of the dockyard workers involved in the project.

★

At a later date a situation arose that spoilt the comradeship of the Rosia Swimming Club committee. With the building in use it was agreed that on Monday evenings committee members would go down to Rosia and brush out and wash the floors of the building and surrounding area.

For a while this went on quite smoothly. Then on several Monday evenings only two persons turned up. I asked the missing committee members if we should change the evening for cleaning the building but they said to leave it as it was. For the following number of Monday evenings there were still only three or sometimes just two of us turning up for the cleaning at Rosia. In the end a number of the committee members resigned, not telling me why they had.

I later found out that these members had joined the Masonic Society and would not disclose that the Masonic meetings were on a Monday evening.

★

The sad occurrence with the Rosia Swimming Club committee made me think about the management problems in the dockyard.

The management structure for ship refitting work was made up as follows. At the head there was a Chief Constructor (Naval Captain's equivalent rank) and below him a Constructor and Naval Officers.

The Constructor was in overall charge of ship refitting and associated machine shops. Below him there were two Foreman of Yards in charge of Inspectors of trades and finally below them individual chargemen.

In the main the Foreman of Yards ran the show and ruled the workplace very strictly. They were classed as "gods" because they controlled how the work was conducted in the North and South Yards.

The one that caused the most problems was Bill Lock the Foreman of the Yard for the North Yard.

He was dictatorial in his attitude to the workforce and the chargemen of the different trades feared him. Because of his dictatorial attitude the Spanish and Gibraltarian workers took a dislike to him.

Some of the workers at this time tried to poison the Foreman of Yard's dog and also stole an electric kettle from his office and hung it over the side of a dry dock! Despite these drawbacks the majority of the workers were loyal and had a good relationship with their chargemen and Inspectors.

Despite the problems and because of the low pay of the workers, as well as a fairly good refitting set-up with dry docks and machine shops, ships were refitted much more cheaply in Gibraltar Dockyard than other dockyards in Britain.

★

Another incident occurred at this time was that a young Inspector of Shipwrights, whose name I will not disclose in case he is still alive, accused the local Gibraltarian workmen of being lazy. This caused an uproar with the local workmen in the dockyard. It ended up with an article being produced in the *Gibraltar Post* newspaper. The top management in the dockyard thought about sending the Inspector back to Britain. They were persuaded not to do that as the young Inspector had published an apology in the *Gibraltar Post* and the atmosphere in the dockyard returned to normal. The Inspector was told that in future he should keep his comments to himself.

★

During 1963 we enjoyed many weekends travelling away from Gibraltar visiting Algeciras, Granada where the beautiful Alhambra Palace was so spectacular, and Fengirola. We even went up into the mountains again to Coin, a quaint old worldy village where we purchased some excellent pottery to take back to our home in Gibraltar. We even visited Estapona again as it was close to Gibraltar and we liked the hotel there. We even got Roy and Margaret Hare to visit Ronda as we knew they would like the picturesque town and valley. Unfortunately I didn't know Margaret Hare was scared of heights and going up and down the dangerous mountain road she had her eyes closed on both of the journeys. Although the roads were poor there wasn't much traffic to worry about and the distances to the towns mentioned were easily accessible by car.

For one week's holiday we stayed in a hotel at Castel del Ferro. To get to it I had to drive a long way along the Spanish coast. On the way the countryside was very bare with little vegetation and large outcrops of volcanic rock. Taking such a long trip was worth it as we stayed in a beautiful hotel with a heated swimming pool in front of the hotel. The hotel was run by a Dutch couple who were most welcoming as they didn't get many visitors being in a remote location. The food, as you can guess, was basically Dutch, but the dinners we had were excellent.

Best of all we swam in the swimming pool every day as it was so warm. Louise loved it and made sure we used the pool as much as possible.

We were sorry to leave such a unique place and return to Gibraltar.

Looking back we were glad we had so many visits to resorts in Spain as it was predicted that the border would probably be closed by the Spanish authorities in the next year 1964.

In the winter of 1962/63 Gibraltar had heavy storms and wet weather. In one period we had nine days of persistent heavy rain. Dockyard families were at a loss what to do especially if they were living in small flats. As you can guess the picture houses were full during that period.

★

One Inspector whose new car had just arrived from Britain was telephoned by the garage. He was told, "Your new car is in the cellar part of the garage and if you don't come and collect it now it will be under water with the heavy rains. The Inspector soon got a lift to the garage and saved his new car from damage.

Other than the storms Margaret and I kept ourselves occupied. Margaret was encouraged to join the Dockyard Ladies Rifle Shooting Club. Although she was reluctant at first having never fired a rifle before she soon got used to the rifle shooting and shot quite well.

The skipper of the team was a Mrs Chipperfield, the wife of a UK welder. Although she was heavily pregnant she still got down on the ground to shoot. She was the best shot in the team despite the inconvenience.

For myself I got up a dockyard table tennis team with two shipwright chargemen. We competed in the Gibraltar Table Tennis League and did reasonably well coming second in the league. The winners were the Bank of Gibraltar Leisure Club who had a strong team as they were able to select their best three players from a large number of staff who played at their Leisure Centre.

In the Civil Service Table Tennis Open competition I was beaten in the final.

At least I won the shove halfpenny competition. I succeeded by always staying on the left-hand side to play right-handed. None of the other players, although right handed, moved me out of the way to play on the left -hand side. So by skill and stealth I was the Gibraltar Shove Halfpenny Champion!

Not to be outdone, Margaret with her partner, a UK engineer off one of the dockyard tugs got to the semi-final of the Naval Open Tennis competition at the Parade Tennis Club. Afterwards she was invited to play at the Royal Parade Club, which incidentally was a select club. Margaret said thank you for the offer to the secretary but preferred to play at the Dockyard Tennis Club as she knew all the members there!

★

After the storms at the beginning of Spring, Margaret and I with some of the tennis club members visited the Dockyard Tennis Club premises. We could not believe how much damage the storm had done to the tennis courts. Most of the surfaces were badly cracked and in some areas parts of the courts had collapsed completely leaving big holes. Even the changing hut was damaged beyond repair. The secretary commented that it was so bad it was too big a job and too costly to repair the courts so we will have to find another venue.

For several weeks Margaret, Louise and I had to be content with visits to the Swimming Club at Rosia.

About six weeks later the secretary of the tennis club called a meeting of the club. We wondered what he had to tell us.

At the meeting he told us that he had obtained the use of a tennis court. Seemingly, the Port Admiral, hearing of the club's plight offered the secretary the use of his own private tennis court.

The court was situated in front of the Port Admiral's house. The house had been erected after a flat area had been created by cutting into the hill above the dockyard. In front of the house was a hollow in the ground where a flat area was excavated large enough to set out one tennis court and a surrounding flat area around the court.

We were all invited to look at the Port Admiral's tennis court the next day. When we arrived at the Port Admiral's residence we had to cross a road and climb down some steps to get to the tennis court in the hollow.

When we looked at the tennis court we found it in excellent condition and may not have been played on much in the previous years.

The surrounding area was unusual with creepers and other vegetation extending from the garden above hanging over the rock face close to the court. There was plenty of room around the court where people could sit on jutting out slabs of rocks. The whole area with its greenery was unique and fascinating especially having a tennis court in the middle of it.

As the secretary said to us, "As you can see there is only one court and there are certain days in the week when we couldn't play on it." We didn't mind that limitation as the club would mainly play at weekends. Also because it was only one court we would have to limit the play to single sets.

From then on the club used the Port Admiral's court quite a lot mainly at weekends. It seemed fascinating to play tennis within these unusual surroundings.

A few months later the Dockyard Works Department found a site for us further along Queensway and built two hard courts and provided a hut for players to use for changing purposes and storage of gear. We had an added advantage because the courts were situated next to the seashore, so, after a game on a hot day, we would take off our shoes and socks and have a paddle in the sea water.

Before the border was closed many of the dockyard workers and staff families used to cross the border taking a tent and camping in the Spanish countryside or on the beach at Algeciras. When the border was closed those families had to find things to do in Gibraltar. It was difficult for those families who didn't play any sports or didn't swim.

At least dockyard families could picnic at Rosia, Camp Bay or Catlan Bay beaches. Although when the border closed these places became at times overcrowded.

At least Gibraltar had two modern picture houses which showed all the latest Hollywood made films. I remember we saw Sean Connery in a Bond film and the *Day of the Triffids* where Gibraltar was mentioned in the film.

★

In the summer of 1963 Margaret's mum and dad decided to fly out to Gibraltar and stay with us for several weeks. It took quite a few letters from Margaret to persuade them to visit us. At first they were reluctant as they had never been out of Britain and never travelled on an aeroplane.

Margaret's mother was very nervous about travelling to a strange country but after much prompting by Margaret's dad was persuaded to make the trip to Gibraltar.

Once it was agreed that they were coming to Gibraltar Margaret's dad fixed his summer holiday with the shipyard he was employed by in Glasgow. He soon had the flight booked and date and time of flight fixed.

As they were due to arrive at Gibraltar Airport late in the afternoon I left the dockyard early and picked up Margaret and Louise and drove to the airport.

The flight was on time and there was little delay for them getting through the customs and passports checks.

They were so pleased to see us especially Louise as she had grown so much since we last saw them in the previous August before we departed for Gibraltar.

After a snack and tea Margaret's mum and dad were affected by the hot day in Gibraltar and jetlag from the flight so went to their bedroom and rested for a couple of hours.

When they came downstairs later they brought us up to date on what was happening in Glasgow and what the family had been doing in the last year.

For a couple of days we stayed in Gibraltar visiting Catalan Bay and the Swimming Club at Rosia. I think it was the first time that Margaret's mum, to our knowledge, had ever been in the sea. The seawater in Gibraltar at this time of year being pleasantly warm made it so tempting for her to enjoy a dip in the sea, especially as parts of Rosia's shore was fairly shallow and safe.

★

As they were staying in Gibraltar for several weeks it was suggested that they take a trip to Tangier. After they agreed to the trip I booked a hotel in Tangier for two nights that was only a short walk from where the *Mons Calpe* berthed at Tangier.

So the following Monday I drove the family down to the port where the passenger ship the *Mons Calpe* was berthed. After not being on board for very long the *Mons Calpe* sailed out of Gibraltar and across the Straits of Gibraltar to Tangier. The trip across was quite pleasant with the sea being calm. When we arrived at the port in Tangier it was an easy walk to our hotel.

On reaching the hotel we were met by a dark-bearded Arab wearing a kaftan that shimmered with the reflection of the sun on the golden threads woven into the kaftan cloth. His dress was topped with a magnificent turban of golden-coloured silk.

He immediately took us to the receptionist and after signing in and producing our passports he showed us to our rooms. After a walk around the port and seeing many strange fishing boats in the harbour we returned to the hotel. We were glad to go to our rooms and get washed and changed as it was still hot outside.

We had an enjoyable dinner where there was a choice of European or Arabic dishes. I was the only one to take a chance and try the Arabic dishes; although they were spicy I quite enjoyed them. As we had an excitable and long day we went to bed early.

After breakfast it was decided to visit the Casbah. It was

quite a long walk through the Casbah's narrow streets. We stopped at one of the shops. We were invited in and the shopkeeper sat us down and gave us mint tea. After some bartering, which the Arabs seemed to like, I purchased a camel stool.

★

Then we continued down through the Casbah. Margaret's mum was a bit afraid of the narrowness and atmosphere of the street. She had a shock as standing in a couple of alcoves were two fierce-looking, tall, dark-skinned Arabs in dark robes staring at her. She was eager to press on and get out of the Casbah. The place had the opposite effect on 'Pop'(Margaret's father) as he looked in all the shops and at the trays of trinkets being displayed by vendors. He even bartered with one of the vendors for six wallets. The vendor had to follow him to the port before accepting Pop's price for the wallets. We ended up back at the hotel after quite an experience going through the Casbah.

After resting in our rooms for several hours we changed and went downstairs to have dinner. This time I kept to the European dishes as did the rest of the family.

Next day we left the hotel and made our way to the Port and climbed aboard the *Mons Calpe*. Within about an hour the ship left Tangier for the voyage to Gibraltar.

At first the weather was calm and we all enjoyed the sunshine on the upper deck. After only an hour out from the Port at Tangier the weather started to change, with really strong winds battering the ship. Soon the ship was rocking so badly that passengers started to feel ill and in some cases were quite sick.

Other than Margaret's mother we didn't seem too affected by the weather. It was different for her as she started to feel ill and became pale and drawn. She was determined not to be sick and sat rigid on the upper deck for the rest of the voyage but was very relieved when the ship reached the port in Gibraltar. Once we got her back to our home she recovered and felt a lot better. She said she would not ever go on a ship again.

★

For the rest of the holiday we stayed most of the time in Gibraltar other than one trip to Algeciras for a picnic on the beach. On the days we stayed at home Margaret's dad, who all the grandchildren in Glasgow called 'Pop' played with Louise for hours, showing and playing games he learnt and played in Glasgow as a child. At the end of their holiday we drove them to the airport. After clearing customs and passport control they said their goodbyes, quite upset at having to leave and not expecting to see us for another two years. We were sure they would have plenty of tales to tell their family and friends when they got back to Glasgow.

Just over a week after Margaret's mum and dad returned to Glasgow we went to the Swimming Gala at Rosia Swimming Club. The event was well organised with ropes that were put out for lanes tied to the raft that was drawn in to the shore. Bunting and flags were draped around the area. There were quite a number of events including those for men and ladies who could swim competitively.

I entered the men's beginners' event as I was not very good at swimming. Although I could do breaststroke I tried to compete by doing front crawl. I didn't do all that well and slapped more than swam but some of the front crawl I did got me second place. The winner who did breaststroke didn't seem a beginner to me.

On the other race Margaret won the ladies' beginners event and all the swimmers were beginners.

A disaster for us was the raft race where three of any family had to make up a raft from cardboard boxes. Margaret, Louise and I started reasonably well with Louise wearing a safety belt in between us. Then our raft started to take in water. We finished last with our soggy raft falling apart.

After the races Margaret, being the chairman's wife, presented the prizes. The men's beginners' race winner got a fair size cup and I got a little one!

★

Afterwards we went to the kiosk where Mr Bruson, a local chargeman of painters in the dockyard served sandwiches and drinks. Mr Bruson took over the running of the kiosk and kitchen about a month after it was built. He was very efficient and served up all types of food and drinks. Although he worked full-time in the dockyard he was able to serve in the kiosk most evenings and weekends.

All the dockyard families enjoyed the Swimming Gala and many said that they hoped that it would be held again next year. Once the committee members had tidied up the site and put the ropes and other gear away in the store we all made our way to our own homes quite content with the success of the Swimming Gala.

★

On the following weekend a near drowning occurred at the Rosia Swimming Club. On that Saturday we prepared some sandwiches and drinks for a picnic and took Louise down to Rosia for the day. While we were having our picnic we could see Bill Kingford, a fellow Inspector of Shipwrights, in the water showing his son how to swim in the shallow end. Without realising it, Bill moved with his son into deeper water. When the son realised the water was much deeper he panicked and clung hold of his father's neck and without realising was holding so tight that he was causing Bill to choke for breath. Finding difficulty in trying to free his son's grip he went under the water. When he came up he shouted to people on the shore, as he was frightened himself, and not a good swimmer.

One of the men bathing and myself being both in swimming trunks quickly swam out and managed to get the boy free from his grip on his father and brought him back to the shore with Bill still gasping for breath following us. Once they were on the shore Bill and his son soon recovered. Afterwards, Bill thanked the two of us, then dressed his son and himself, and went home. We hoped that the incident would not put the boy off learning to swim.

At the end of 1963 there was not much going on socially and too early to prepare for Christmas. One day Jim Jeffreys, one of the UK chargemen of shipwrights came up to the Inspectors' Office and asked if Margaret and I would like a trip to Jerez and the Bodega there. It was a town not far from Cadiz.

First of all I said that we could not go as our daughter Louise was too young to take on that sort of trip although we would have liked to go. When Roy Hare who was an

Inspector in the same office was asked if he was interested he said he wasn't interested in that sort of trip.

Luckily Margaret Hare had heard later from her husband about the trip to Jerez and our problem with Louise being too young. She contacted my wife and offered to look after Louise for the weekend. Margaret took up the offer as our daughter knew the Hares very well and had played with her on many occasions when they visited our house.

There were about four couples from the dockyard going on the trip and Jim Jeffreys having visited the Bodega in Jerez before said he would take us in his car. So on the Saturday morning we took Louise down to the Hares' house, which was only a short walk down the slope. We said we would be late back on Sunday to collect her.

Later Jim Jeffreys with his wife picked us up and he drove to the meeting place at the Parade and met the other couples with their cars.

The husbands of the couple who would be driving their cars discussed the route with Jim and were satisfied with the choice he suggested. Jim drove off first followed by the other cars. They all drove fairly carefully as the roads were bad and they had plenty of time to make Jerez before it was dark. All the cars arrived in Jerez about the same time. Jim who had booked the pensions for the group indicated the particular pension for each couple.

★

Jim took us all to a restaurant he had visited before and we had an excellent dinner. Afterwards everyone was feeling tired so we all made our way to our respective pensions.

We found our pension quite comfortable but small, it

only had a single bedroom, shower and small kitchen that we used to make some tea. We slept quite well in the pension and in the morning we had tea but didn't have anything to eat as pensions don't provide that facility.

All the couples met in the square near the Bodega and after chatting for a few minutes made our way to the Bodega. There we were met by one of the staff of the Bodega who welcomed us to the premises. Inside we could catch the smells of the different wines as we walked to the main part of the building.

The staff member started off by giving us all tastes of fino, a light wine, the next taste was a bit stronger than the fino. As we walked through the Bodega we were given more tastes of wine until we ended up tasting a dark strong wine called olerosa. At the end of the long tasting session we thanked the member of staff and most of us bought some wine that we liked. On coming out of the building as it was much later in the day the heat of the sun hit us as well as the large intake of wine with the tasting. As we walked across, or rather staggered across the road, we discovered we were quite tipsy mainly because we hadn't had anything to eat since the dinner the previous evening.

We made our way to the nearest restaurant as quickly as possible to get some food inside us to absorb the intake of wine. Sitting in the restaurant, hungrily eating our meal, we looked across at Jim Jeffreys who was grinning all over his face. We shook our fists at him as he knew what this situation, with the absence of food, would do when taking so much wine since he had visited the Bodega before. After our meal we had a walk around the town to see the old buildings and to complete the sobering up.

By the late afternoon we were all on our way back to Gibraltar having enjoyed the company and the trip with only the slightest of headaches. On reaching Gibraltar Jim Jeffreys dropped us off at our house and left after we thanked him for taking us to Jerez.

We walked across to the Hares' house which was only down the slope from our house and knocked on their door. The Hares invited us in and asked how the trip went for us, which we said we enjoyed. As it was late, they said after having a cup of tea that Louise was asleep and that Margaret could collect her on Monday morning.

While we were drinking our tea, Margaret Hare told us that she had something important to tell us and that was she was pregnant. It would be their first child especially as they were an older couple. We congratulated them on their news and made our way back to our own home quite content with the trip to Jerez.

Quite soon after our trip Margaret had a check-up with the doctor and found she was pregnant. We were pleased because we wanted a son as we already had a daughter.

It was not long after Margaret's news of her pregnancy coming out that Gordon Bowring's wife was found to be also pregnant. Gordon was another Inspector of Shipwrights in our office. Fancy three pregnancies of wives of husbands all working in the same office – quite a coincidence. It must have been the hot weather or what?

★

At the end of 1963 and at the beginning of 1964 other than the long refit of HMS *Carysford* at the North Yard we only had the refit of spare caissons and some barges.

During these quiet periods shipwrights and other constructive trades were transferred from the caisson refits to the refit of HMS *Carysford* when there was an increase in structural work at certain stages of the refit.

When any of the Inspectors of Shipwrights on HMS *Carysford* refit were sick or on leave I would stand in for them.

★

Although there was less work to do in the ship refitting areas of the North Yard the machine shops were very busy. HMS *Carysford* was at a stage where the accommodation and other lower deck spaces were being fitted out so there was a great demand for the manufacture of metal trunks and fittings for ventilation and air conditioning also demands on coppersmith and plumber shops for pipework to be fitted at the ship.

The Blacksmiths Shop was tasked with testing all the anchor and cable arrangements and associated gear for HMS *Carysford*. This was quite a task for a small Blacksmiths Shop. Despite its size, the work was carried out quite efficiently by the blacksmiths under the UK chargeman named Charlie Stair who hailed from Portsmouth Dockyard. As HMS *Carysford* was the major refit in the dockyard it naturally had priority for items being manufactured in all the Shops in order to achieve a completion date in May 1964.

★

At the beginning of 1964 I was tasked to travel back to Britain to examine the state of HMS *Cavalier* in Devonport Dockyard. HMS *Cavalier* was due to sail to Gibraltar if her engine and boiler seatings and associated structure were not too badly corroded as the repair would need the engines and boilers to be lifted out, a huge task, so that the structural repairs could be undertaken.

I went to the main office and picked up my tickets for the flight to Brize Norton. A naval car took me to the airport where I climbed on the Dakota aeroplane which was not the most comfortable plane to fly in. There were several families on the aeroplane going back to Britain. Families who were staying in Gibraltar for a three-year tour were allowed concessionary flights back to Britain to see other members of family there. The flight first of all went reasonably well although, like all the Dakotas, was bumpy. Soon we hit a storm and the aeroplane was shaking with the wind. Sometimes there was changes in the wind and the aeroplane dropped hundreds of feet.

At this stage some of the members of the families were sick. Although I didn't like flying I only felt a little queasy but recovered when the pilot climbed the Dakota to a safer height clear of the storm. When we landed at Brize Norton there was a sigh of relief from the passengers.

At Brize Norton I was taken by car to the station for my train and travelled to London where I caught a train at Paddington which took me to Plymouth North Road Station. Then it was a short walk to the hotel I was booked into for one or two nights. I had an evening meal at the hotel and then decided to have an early night and go to bed.

After breakfast I got a naval car to Devonport Dockyard. There I had to go to the Main Office to get a security pass that allowed me to go on board HMS *Cavalier* which was tied up at a berth in the harbour within the Saint Levens Road area of the dockyard.

At the security gate of the fence that surrounded HMS *Cavalier* I was met by a naval officer who showed me around the ship. After some discussion with the officer I borrowed a set of overalls and climbed down to the engine room and had a thorough examination of the huge engine seatings and surrounding linked structure and then moved on to the large boiler seatings and linked structure.

I found both seatings and linked structures in good condition and just needed a wire brushing and a coat of paint. I then went up to the drawing office to collect structural drawings of HMS *Cavalier*.

While I was in the drawing office I met draughtsmen who had been in the same shipwright apprenticeship as myself at Devonport Dockyard. Where I had passed an examination for an Inspector of Trades they had been content to pass examinations to become draughtsmen. While I was chatting to them I noticed on another bench some drawings that showed proposals for additional concrete blocks to improve the large dry dock facilities for docking various sized ships.

★

Knowing that Gibraltar had large dry docks I asked the leading draughtsman in charge of the section if the docking improvements were going to be adopted at Devonport Dockyard. He replied that contracts had already gone out for shaped concrete blocks to be manufactured to install them in No 1 Dock.

I asked if I could get a copy of the drawings but he said that I would have to get permission from the design section at MOD Headquarters at Bath to release copies of drawings to take back to Gibraltar.

With my task complete at Devonport I took the train to Bath and then a bus to Comb Down where the MOD Headquarters was sited in various single storey blocks. There I got entry and went to see the Chief Draughtsman who dealt with the large dock modifications. When I met and introduced myself and explained why I was in Britain I asked if I could take copies of the proposed modifications for a large dock back to Gibraltar, as these same modifications could be undertaken in Gibraltar Dockyard as it had a similar large dock to the one in Devonport Dockyard. Once the Chief Draughtsman agreed to my request he sent one of his draughtsmen to make copies of the drawings for me to take away.

Being at Headquarters in Bath I knew that Gordon Bowring had just been promoted to an acting naval constructor at MOD Headquarters in Bath having not many weeks before been an Inspector of Shipwrights on HMS *Carysford's* refit in Gibraltar.

Once I had the drawings I went to Gordon Bowring's section which was only in the next block. After a chat we went to the canteen and ate a meal together. In the canteen he told me what he was doing in his new post. We decided to meet at the hotel, which the clerical office had booked for me, for a drink, .

★

I was glad to get away and go to the hotel as climbing under the engine and boiler seatings I ended up with dirty clothes and got sweaty. At the hotel I showered and changed and had dinner in the hotel. Later Gordon Bowring came to the hotel and we had a few drinks in the lounge. He told me that he was finding it difficult to buy a house to suit his finances even though he'd had a rise in pay. Unfortunately he had previously sold his house in Chatham and while he was several years away in Gibraltar the price of houses had risen dramatically. He said that he and his wife was settled in a flat in Bath and was not too far distant from her relatives. Before we departed he said he would keep in contact with me.

The next morning I collected the dock drawings from a locked cupboard and, with them and my bag, made my way to the station.

My return journey to Gibraltar was uneventful although the returning Dakota aeroplane still shook a lot. I returned home quite pleased with my trip to Britain and what had transpired. Not only was HMS *Cavalier* saved from being scrapped it had a successful refit in Gibraltar.

In latter years HMS *Cavalier*, although quite old, was saved again from being scrapped and was made a museum piece for visitors to go on board and see an example of this type of ship built in the 1950s. As regards the drawings of the dock block modifications I took them to my Foreman of Yard Bill Lock who was quite pleased with my ingenuity to find the drawings being used in Devonport. He also said, "Well done getting the information on HMS *Cavalier*." He took the drawings to his Naval Constructor David Moss who was taken with the proposed modification to a large dry dock.

Several months later the dock block modifications were carried out in Gibraltar's No 1 Dock. It had been worthwhile getting the drawings from the MOD Headquarters section in Bath.

Early in January 1964 after most of the festivities were over I was at a loose end. After serving my year as a chairman of the Rosia Swimming Club committee I had handed the chairmanship over to an Electrical Inspector with a reasonable club bank balance due to the good work of our treasurer. I was not expecting to join any further organisations.

Margaret and I were invited to a paid buffet supper at the Dockyard Social Club by Ken Chipperfield and his wife. After entering the club and paying for our tickets Ken and I went for drinks from the bar. Seemingly there was a row going on at the bar, one of the UK workmen had been stealing drinks and even drinking some of other men's partly drunk pints. He was renowned for this offence. This time the bar manager ordered the workman out of the premises.

After taking the drinks to my wife and Rose Chipperfield we settled down at a table to listen to the mandolin player from Catalan Bay. He played a number of Italian songs which all the members there enjoyed. After the mandolin player had finished we all made our way to the tables laid out with sandwiches and savouries. When we had eaten our food and were chatting the chairman of the Social Club got up and thanked us all for coming to the buffet supper. He explained that the proceeds of tonight's supper would go into the very depleted funds. He asked if anyone had any ideas for making some money for the Social Club. There were a few suggestions but they were not taken up. Someone suggested a dance with a bar. Me and my big mouth said I would help to organise a dance and a few others offered their help but pointed at me to be the organiser of the dance, knowing how much I had done for the Rosia Swimming Club.

Although when we lived in Dunfermline in Fife we went to many dances including ones for charity I did not know how to run a dance. Anyway the people who volunteered and I met a few days later. By then I had some thoughts on hiring a band and a hall for the dance. The others volunteered for different jobs like doorkeeper to collect the money or serving behind the bar.

★

The next week I made enquiries and managed to book a hall and a dance band for the end of January. The "bush telegraph" must have been working as a bongo three-piece bandleader contacted me and offered to play on the same nights for free in order to get publicity for their night club in downtown Gibraltar which I accepted. With this fixed I went back to the wine and spirits firm that I had previously done business with and ordered a sensible selection of drinks to sell at our bar at the dance.

At the next stage I organised the production of tickets with an entry fee of five shillings. On the tickets we had put no drinks were to be brought into the dance, as we wanted the money to swell the funds of the Social Club.

When we received the tickets every member of the Social Club made an effort to sell them and we managed to sell at least fifty tickets right away.

On the day of the dance with the help of the wives of the members the hall was decorated with flags and streamers and looked quite attractive. With the arrival of the alcoholic drinks we set up a bar with trestles and covered them with white paper and placed them at the end of the hall. We marked out two areas for the bands and set out tables and chairs around the hall. That evening the dance bands came early and were set up and playing before many of the ticket holders had come into the hall. The member doing the doorkeeping and ticket collecting was doing a good job. He stopped most of the people still deciding to bring alcohol into the dance and asked them to leave them with him as he said to them that bringing in and using their own bottles would lose money at the bar which the Club desperately needed. Despite this request some of the ticket holders still got away with small bottles of drink.

Most of the evening I was serving behind the bar but I had a few dances with Margaret. The dance seemed to be going quite well as the bar was well used. That is until an incident happened when I went to collect empty glasses from the Inspector of Fitters from the dockyard at a table. He seemed the worse for drink and said to me that the dance bands were rotten. I didn't notice him dancing! Bill Lock whose wife was sitting with him just grinned at his remarks. He had quite a lot of drink himself.

After working so hard organising the dance and working all day in the hall I was quite tired and angry at the Inspector of Fitter's remarks and stepped over to his table to punch him in the jaw. As I got to the table the other person at the bar, who was the one who beat me in the swimming race for beginners, saw the situation and quickly came over and grabbed my arm and led me back to the bar to allow me to cool down. The chap who stopped me having a set-to was an Inspector of Electricians, a very nice person to be associated with and I worked with him in latter years in Rosyth Dockyard.

Despite the problem with the Inspector of Fitters the dance went well and we made, with people also contributing money as well as the bar takings, over one hundred pounds for the Social Club – quite a sum in those days.

As regards the incident with the Inspector of Fitters, I never remembered his name, the bad feeling between us had been growing over a long period. It started when I was the Inspector of the Constructive Shops and he had the Mechanical Shops. During the first year I got my bid in for my holiday leave in early for the prime time in the summer when unfortunately he had to look after my Shops while I was away on holiday. I didn't know that this would happen but he felt that I did know and I didn't consider him at all.

Hence on many occasions we had problems when we passed each other's paths on jobs on various ships. One particular problem occurred on the *Ark Royal* project. Some scaffolding had to be erected in the evening on the ship's side. I had returned home to get something to eat that evening but because Margaret had to go out for a small bore shooting match I was delayed getting my daughter Louise ready to take with me back to the dockyard. When I got there a bit late there was the Inspector of Fitters waiting for me and said to me that I was late for the erection of the scaffolding. Although there wasn't any delay to the job he was pleased to have a go at me for being late.

★

The next morning he came up to the Inspectors' Office and had a go at me about being late the previous evening in the dockyard. This started another row between us and got quite heated especially in front of the other Inspectors in the office. Before it got any worse, Bill Lock, hearing the fierce argument called me into his office which was next to ours and calmed me down. He told the other Inspectors to get rid of the Inspector of Fitters from the office. So you see the trouble at the dance all stemmed from him not getting his holiday when he wanted it the previous year.

★

In March 1964 HMS *Cavalier* sailed to Gibraltar and was tied up at a berth in the harbour. At the berth all the loose fittings and equipment was removed in readiness to move into dry dock at the start of its long refit similar to that of HMS *Carysford* due to complete in May. Also in March David Ross, the Naval Constructor, returned to Britain after his three-year tour. Ray Strickland took his place and soon settled into his job.

One task he wanted to follow up was to go aboard HMS *Cavalier* and examine the engine and boiler seatings to satisfy himself that they were as in such a good condition as I detailed in my report on HMS *Cavalier*. He rang up Bill Lock and asked to have a look at HMS *Cavalier* especially the engine and boiler seatings. Bill Lock replied that this could be arranged. He fixed to have me meet Mr Strickland that afternoon at two o'clock at the ship. Just before two o'clock I walked over to HMS *Cavalier* taking two sets of overalls for Mr Strickland and myself.

At two o'clock Mr Strickland was waiting for me at the gangway leading to HMS *Cavalier*. He introduced himself and so did I and after putting on the overalls we went on board. After first looking through the ship we climbed down to the engine room where Mr Strickland examined the seatings thoroughly and did the same with the boiler seatings.

After his examinations he was pleasantly surprised seeing the seatings in such a good condition considering it was an old ship. On leaving the ship he gave me the overalls he used and thanked me for my time and said he agreed wholeheartedly with my report. Apart from the work he asked me how I was enjoying life in Gibraltar. I gave him a rundown of what my wife and I were doing in Gibraltar.

I found him easy to talk to and seemed quite a pleasant person. I felt sure that the Inspectors and Foremen would also find him easy to get on with at work.

★

Although it was Spring Margaret and I were still involved in our own sports. Later on, as she was getting bigger as a result of being six or seven months pregnant, she gave up the small bore shooting and I gave up playing table tennis. Instead we took a few trips to Catalan Bay and sat on the beach and had picnics when the weather was not too cold. Other times we would go with Louise down to the Rosia Swimming Club.

With the baby expected at the end of May, I wrote to Margaret's sister Betty McCormick in Glasgow and asked her if she wouldn't mind coming out to Gibraltar and being a companion for Margaret after the baby was born. She wrote back and said she would be delighted to. It would also be a bit of a holiday as well since she still had to care for her son Ronald who was about the same age as Louise.

★

At the end of May, Margaret who was now due to have the baby within the next few days, was taken into the Naval Hospital where they would keep an eye on her as the birth was overdue. I had taken leave to look after Louise and didn't go far from the house except for purchasing groceries. Sometimes we would go over to the Hares' house and have tea. While Margaret was still in hospital Margaret's sister arrived with young Ronald and settled in. It was a bonus for Louise as she would now have Ronald to play with.

On the 25th May our son Mark was born; he had fair skin and black hair, completely different colouring from Louise who had red hair. Margaret didn't have any complications but was very tired with the birth. I brought her back after she had been in the hospital for another three days. For the next few days Margaret just rested at home mainly chatting with her sister about what was happening with the family in Glasgow.

Once Margaret felt better we all went in the car to Europa Point to see the lighthouse and look out over miles of deep blue sea. The following day we took food and drink and had a picnic at the Rosia Swimming Club. Margaret soon felt stronger after a few more days sitting on the veranda of our house, enjoying the warm sunshine and talking to Betty. The next day, as Margaret felt stronger, we took the car and drove across the Spanish border to Algeciras where we sunbathed on the beach. As the water was warm the children got their swimming costumes on and played in the water. At the end of the second week before Betty returned to Glasgow we took the car and went across the Spanish border to La Linea where Betty bought quite a number of presents to take back for the family in Glasgow.

It would be the last time we visited Algeciras or La Linea as not long after our visits the Spanish authorities closed the border.

This was a blow for many UK workers' families as many of them up to then were used to taking tents at weekends and enjoying the freedom of the Spanish countryside just a few miles from the Spanish border. Soon after the La Linea and Algeciras visits, Betty and her son returned to Glasgow taking back the many gifts for her family.

A few weeks after Margaret's sister returned to Glasgow Margaret Hare went into hospital where she had a baby girl who was named Alison. When Margaret Hare came out of hospital with Alison, my wife and I went to see them at their nearby home. From then on we visited them quite often and they often came to our house.

Unfortunately Alison didn't sleep very well at night so Margaret and her husband Roy had to take in turns sitting up with the baby on many nights. On several occasions we invited them across to our home for a drink. When they did come to our house on those evenings Alison was still wide awake in her pram. Sometimes to try and get Alison to sleep Roy would give her a teaspoon of wine but it didn't work.

A few months later Roy was offered a post back in Newcastle MOD Ship Building Overseeing Group which he accepted so that they could get back to Newcastle and stay near Margaret Hare's family and friends. They never properly settled in Gibraltar and Roy still had over a year of his tour to serve. Margaret and I felt they could have seen a lot more of Spain before their daughter was born. They were good friends of ours and we certainly missed them after they returned to Newcastle.

When I returned to work after paternal leave I was kept quite busy. In North Yard we had a series of dockings and undockings of caissons and a number of small ships and tugs. That meant I was the dockmaster in each case and therefore exposed to strong sunlight. I didn't wear a hat as I didn't think with having thick hair that I needed one seeing all the shipwrights on the docking and undockings were bare-headed.

At the end of a couple of weeks I started to get headaches and tended to bow my head to avoid the worst of the sun. My headache got worse and I went to the Naval Doctor who said I had sunstroke and sent me home. After something to eat I went and lay on my bed and Margaret closed the curtains and darkened the room. I was kept in the dark for a couple of days until I felt the headaches lessen and gradually go away.

★

I returned to work the following day wearing a hat to be on the safe side although I didn't have any dockings to be present at for a few weeks as all the small ships and caissons were now afloat and workmen were busy with repairs on board these vessels. Although walking around I was still crouching with my head down as I hadn't got out of this habit with the sun. I was told that I would be kept off dockings for a while just to be on the safe side. The experience had taught me a lesson about not looking after myself.

One day when I was walking around the dockside I heard

a Spanish worker pointing at me and saying "hubago". I didn't know what he meant so I walked along and asked the workman's chargeman what the word meant. He explained that the word "hubago" meant hunchback. I think it was the way I walked as I bent my head and body.

Funny how you acquire nicknames. Others of the UK staff had nicknames: Gordon Bowring was called "strip" as on a ship repair he kept on that where there were holes in the deck that the chargeman should put steel strips over the holes.

David Moss because he was very tall and gaunt was called "streak". Bill Lock was called the "kettle man" after the workers stole his kettle. Roy Hare was called "leveret" – Spanish for a small hare.

I am sure there are other UK staff who had nicknames, so would the UK chargeman who sold illicit bottles of wine be called "the smuggler?"

So with less work in the North Yard I didn't have to work any of the weekends so Margaret, Louise, baby Mark and I went down to the Rosea Swimming Club quite often where I could take turns with Margaret and do some swimming. As well, Louise enjoyed playing in the paddling pool. With the club being used by UK dockyard workers and staff there was always someone we would meet and talk to. While not working weekends Margaret and I were able to go to one or two cocktail parties.

In the autumn we were invited to several parties mostly near our own house. We had an excellent babysitter called Anne Fisher who was the daughter of a UK Inspector of Engine Fitters in the dockyard who we knew very well having been to cocktail parties with them. Anne Fisher had a part-time job in a shop in the town centre but she was poorly paid so she was glad of the money from babysitting jobs.

One party we were invited to required wearing fancy dress, Margaret borrowed a beautiful sari dress from an Indian lady we knew. I had a plain blue pair of pyjamas and made a coolie hat and a moustache. One older woman who I danced with had a strange witch's fancy dress; while dancing she said she fancied me with a gleam in her eye. I was taken aback and said no thank you. She was old enough to be my "grannie". Despite that embarrassment we had a great time at the party.

In the summer of 1964 HMS *Cavalier,* after the removal of her loose equipment and redundant fittings, went into dry dock. I talked to the new Inspector of Shipwrights, whose desk was in the Inspectors' Office, about the state of the ship. He replied that after the hull was shot-blasted it was found that a large amount of steel plating would have to be removed because it was badly corroded and new steel plating would have to be welded in its place. While in dock the ship was swarming with Constructive, Electrical and Mechanical trades. The large numbers were required so that all the fittings and equipment would be removed and sent back to the Shops for overhaul, modification or replacement if beyond economic repair. Doing this would give an early start to the large package of work the Shops would have to undertake. It was essential that this equipment and fittings were repaired, modified or replaced in as short a time as possible. The prompt return of equipment and fittings would give the different trades time enough to fit and test this equipment and fittings to meet the completion date of HMS *Cavalier's* long refit. Once the bulk of the early constructive work was complete it would free up workmen for other tasks in the North Yard. Freeing this labour would allow the management to take on the refit of Rand Shipping Company's passenger ferry. Normally this vessel would have been refitted in the South Yard but as the South Yard was overloaded with work the contract was passed to the North Yard.

Although the passenger ferry was smaller than the *Mons Calpe* it was in a worse condition. It needed considerable hull repairs and its decking and upper deck wooden timber fittings were needing quite a lot of renewal. At least having this contract gave the constructive trades such as shipwrights, welders, joiners and other associated workmen plenty of work for quite a long time. As the ship's refit period was quite long the constructive trades could balance the work on board and therefore not have to employ large numbers of each trade.

I was in charge of this refit and it was a joy to see a sad-looking ship suddenly start to look better as work progressed.

At the end of the refit you would not believe the change that had taken place with the new deckings, wood timbers and brass fittings completed. The passenger ferry looked nearly brand new again!

★

At the beginning of 1965 I had my worst experience with something going wrong at a ship's refit. It happened when the North Yard was refitting a dockyard support vessel.

I was in charge of the refit of the support ship. We didn't know how bad a state the ship was in until we got her in dry dock. Many of the valves and fittings to the hull had to be removed and replaced. On board a considerable number of pipework systems had to be repaired and new valves and controls fitted.

As we were not allowed a long period in dry dock shipwrights, caulkers and welders had to take on a heavy load in the time given. A large number of hull steel plates had to be replaced where the hull was badly corroded. After working for weeks including weekends, the steel plating replacement and painting was finished just before the ship undocked. At the end of the refit there was a smaller corroded area just above the waterline that had to be repaired, so using only one welder on a small staging, the welder got his gear up on to the top of the staging to undertake the repair. He had to chip the corroded area and make a weld repair as it was too small for the corroded area to be removed and be replaced by a steel plate.

To be on the safe side I asked the acting chargeman (the main chargeman was away on another job) to check the compartment inside where the welding was to take place. He went on board and did a check and then told me that the compartment was clear of any combustible materials or liquids.

When I got the clearance by the chargeman I gave the welder the go-ahead and he started chipping off the corrosion on that area of the hull. Once he cleared the corrosion he struck the welding rod on the thin area of steel plate which caused a small hole to appear in the chipped area. Suddenly there was a burst of flame as it ignited oil seeping through the hole. Luckily the force of the oil pouring out through the hole, which got bigger with the pressure of the oil, put out the flame caused by the struck electrode stick.

If the oil pouring out had caught on fire or if there was gas in the compartment there could have been an explosion and the welder might have been badly injured. What I didn't know when I gave the order to start welding the corroded area was that the acting chargeman had been checking the wrong compartment! Actually he should have been checking the compartment that had been used for holding a large amount of oil.

There I was, standing on the dockside counting my blessings that we could have had an explosion if gas had been present. Then as I looked into the dry dock I could see a pool of oil forming on the dock floor. The oil still poured out of the ship and poured, and poured until there was a very large pool of oil on the dock floor. I realised it was a bit of a crisis as I knew we could not undock on the following Monday with the ship pouring out oil. Therefore I had to go and see the Foreman of the Yard, Bill Lock. As it was a Saturday he wasn't happy to be disturbed. I told him about the oil leak and he blew his top and said because the acting chargeman on duty was not the same calibre as the main chargeman, I should have checked the compartment.

When we went down to the dockside the situation looked worse as there was a huge pool of oil on the dock floor and the oil was still pouring out. So he had to go off and tell the Naval Constructor about the oil in the dock that needed to be cleared; the remaining oil in the compartment had to be pumped out and the compartment needed to be ventilated and checked that it was gas-free.

This work took about a week to complete especially

because of having to bring in a tanker to pump out the rest of the oil. Was I glad to see the corroded area and hole welded at the end of the following week and painted, then relieved to see the ship undocked and steamed away to her usual berth. It was a sad experience for me and it taught me a lesson. If ever it happened again I would make sure myself that a compartment was clear for welding to take place.

In March 1965 our Foreman of Yard returned to Britain after serving his three-year tour. Many of the staff and workmen were not sorry to see him go. He was replaced by Mr King – what a difference in personality. He was quite approachable and would listen to any problem and give a sensible solution. I found after a while he would be ideal to work with in the North Yard.

During the next month an ideal project came up that I would have liked to take on but I didn't know if the disaster on the support vessel would stop me getting the project. I was quite surprised when I did get the project. I found out afterwards that Mr King had made enquiries about me and was told that I did an excellent job on HMS *Ark Royal* and the nuclear submarine HMS *Dreadnought*.

I was tasked with a very interesting project. An old destroyer had been brought into the dockyard to have the whole of its accommodation refurbished. After it had been brought into the harbour at Gibraltar it was moved to a berth in the dockyard. I climbed aboard and walked through the ship. The accommodation was in a very poor state with paintwork quite dirty and peeling off. The decks were covered with the old-style dark brown cortisene, that would be replaced by the modern PVC linoleum, and was holed in many places. The messes looked worse for wear with much of the furniture broken and lockers in many cases still constructed of wood.

I wondered how to plan the refurbishment so I talked to one of the older Inspectors of Shipwrights who had experience in refitting accommodation when he worked in Devonport Dockyard. He advised me that I should start at the fore end of the ship and work my way aft and out of the ship.

So going on board I started at the fore end where there were storage lockers and racks for ship's equipment and noted the repairs that were needed. Then aft to the seamen's mess and then on to the higher ranks' messes. From there I progressed to the officers' quarters. In each area I jotted down in my notebook the repairs and alterations needed in these spaces.

Once I had taken in the whole picture of refurbishment needed I sat down in the office and assessed the total workload needed for the painters, shipwrights, joiners and other trades. The total estimate I present to Mr King the Foreman of the Yard who accepted my proposed workload.

One major difficulty I had to work out was how to balance the use of painters and other trades in congested areas. In some cases because of the congestion tradesmen had to take in turns who went into these congested areas. For example in one area the painters went in first to paint the area and then the shipwrights to fit new ventilation trunks followed by the joiners to put the final furnishings.

I made a plan based on what I had assessed so that over many weeks the use of tradesmen were sensibly allocated in all the accommodation areas without causing a backlog of work for individual groups of tradesmen. In most cases the work went well other than a few cases where the sequence of work hadn't been adhered to, but these were minor and with working backshifts in these cases the congestion problems were solved.

With the completion of the project the Foreman of the Yard inspected the refurbished accommodation and was pleased with the finished project. It was pleasing to see the new PVC linoleum washed and sparkling as well as many of the accommodation units replaced in shiny aluminium.

I was quite pleased with the execution of the project although I had to spend long hours each week making sure the progress throughout the ship moved on smoothly.

★

At the beginning of June we went to the Church of Scotland Hall where the minister there christened our son giving him Christian names Mark Richard. The Christian name Richard is the same as my second Christian name. The name Richard both of us liked. The name is linked to the Toye family as my grandmother's original surname was Richard. She, like the Toyes, grew up in Cornwall. The church was housed in a long tin-hut-like building. Margaret and I used to attend the church occasionally on a Sunday, although I was not very religious since my mother died in her fifties of cancer after a long painful period of illness. I still went with Margaret as she enjoyed the services and liked the minister who took them.

One of the things I did enjoy was meeting families other than those connected with the dockyard. Many of the families who attended the services were from the Army and Royal Air Force bases. After every service tea was laid on and this enabled us to talk to many of these families and find out how they were faring in Gibraltar and get information on what was happening back in Britain.

The Saturday after the christening Margaret and I were invited to the Church of Scotland minister's home for tea and cakes. After we arrived and settled down in his home we found out that he was older than he looked and was seemingly very fit for his age. He served in the Army during the 1914-1918 World War and won the Military Cross. He told us many stories of his life and made it very interesting. We reciprocated by telling him what we did in Scotland before coming to Gibraltar. It was a breath of fresh air talking to him since among the dockyard families talk was usually related to accommodation problems and other dockyard matters.

★

In the summer many of our UK-based friends returned to Britain after completing their three-year tours. Although we didn't go to any more cocktail or other parties we still played some tennis at the Dockyard Tennis Club and made constant trips to the Rosia Swimming Club, With the Spanish Border still closed any trips had to be local ones.

In August when I was due to return to Britain after my three-year tour I had expected to hand over my duties to a Mr Watson who actually lived not far from our original home in Dunfermline but he was allowed to sail his yacht from Britain to Gibraltar and therefore would arrive after I had gone back to Britain. As I had recently finished the Destroyer project I asked if I could take the week's leave I had left and stay in Gibraltar for that time.

When it was time to leave I said my goodbyes to Mr King and many of the UK chargemen I had worked with during those three years.

So, being free from work, we prepared food and drink and visited various resorts in Gibraltar such as Camp Bay and Catalan Bay as well as our regular one Rosia. We enjoyed spending all day in each of the places mentioned but Catalan Bay we enjoyed the most as it had a large safe beach and was often not very busy. It was a joy to see our daughter Louise and baby son Mark, fifteen months old running freely around the beach. In the case of Mark it was more of a stagger than running! At the same time that I got permission to stay that week in Gibraltar we opted to return to Britain by sea rather than the usual flight home to London and Edinburgh.

Well before we left Gibraltar I had booked on a cargo/passenger ship sailing to Liverpool which would take four and a half days.

We had to pack a couple of large packing cases with our large items that would go in a pound ready to go on the cargo/passenger ship we were to sail on. In addition our car had to be put in the pound so that it could be stowed on board long before we went on board.

When our departure was due the Inspector of Shipwrights on the refit of HMS *Cavalier* offered to take us and our belongings down to the ship. He was a quiet man who didn't get on with his Foreman of Yard, Bill Lock, and stood up to him when there were arguments. He was of stern stuff and although just a little younger than Bill Lock seemed to know a bit more about shipbuilding and ship repair than him and so he was able to stand his ground in any arguments. Although I didn't know the Inspector that well and I cannot remember his name I found him easy to get along with at work.

On the departure day he picked us and our belongings up and took us to the ship. On unloading ourselves and belongings we thanked him for his help and he drove off.

★

On board we were given two cabins, a larger one for Margaret and the children and a smaller one for me. We found them to be quite comfortable. On board during the day we had regular meals in one of the messes. At night we had dinner in part of the officers' accommodation. At dinner we had the company of Peter Yaun and his wife. They were returning to Britain at the same time as us after he had completed his three-year tour as a Senior Draughtsman in the Main Office.

The passage across to Liverpool was excellent as it was quite calm for the whole of the voyage. We missed the rough seas that are sometimes experienced when going across the Bay of Biscay. On arrival at Liverpool I picked up the car after it had been lowered on to the berth and with Margaret and the children drove off to Scotland to stay in Dunfermline with friends before starting work in Rosyth Dockyard, and looking for a house to rent.

★

If anyone asked me what I had gained after three years in Gibraltar I would say that my wife and I had gained a wealth of knowledge and experience after living in another country. But more important than that having arrived in Gibraltar with a baby girl left with a bonny little girl and a baby son to enjoy with my wife our life together in the future.

FOUND OUT

Bill Turnbull	Salesman
Dr Linda Smith	Health Clinic Doctor
Dr Rose Thomson	Health Clinic Doctor
June Thornton	Receptionist
Grace Paterson	Patient
Jim Muir	New Salesman

Chapter One

Dr Linda Smith and Dr Rose Thomson own a health clinic in Edinburgh that specialises in alternative medical practices such as acupuncture.

Both doctors are in their early thirties, good-looking and unmarried. Although wanting to settle down at present they enjoy socialising and dating men, though their relationships are always of short duration, that is until a salesman Bill Turnbull visits their premises. He is there to persuade them to purchase medical equipment that his firm specialises in.

Bill is thirty years old, tall, well built, handsome with Scandinavian-like features. He is well spoken with a soft Inverness-shire accent. He is very confident and able to charm most women. Recently he had been left a large sum of money by a relative.

With this legacy he has purchased a modern flat in the Queen Street area of Edinburgh. He has had numerous girlfriends in Edinburgh since he moved from Inverness several years ago.

On entering the Health Clinic Bill Turnbull approached the receptionist June Thornton. After showing her his business card he asked if he could see one of the doctors indicated on the board behind her.

★

The receptionist calls on the intercom to Dr Smith who is the senior member at the clinic to find out if she will see the salesman. As she is free that morning and a little bored she says to the receptionist, "June, will you ask the salesman what goods his firm sells?" June, after asking Mr Turnbull replies, "He represents a company called Foster Brooks that sells specialised medical equipment."

On hearing the reply, Dr Smith asks June to bring Mr Turnbull along to her room. June leads the salesman along the corridor to Dr Smith's room.

She knocks and opens the door to the doctor's room and introduces the salesman. "This is Mr Turnbull to see you."

Dr Smith looks up from her desk and smiles and says, "Please sit down, I believe you represent the firm of Foster Brooks." She has a good look at the salesman and finds him very pleasing to the eye.

The salesman after sitting down says to Dr Smith, "Please do call me Bill."

After passing the time of day Bill Turnbull opens his large case and shows her his wide range of specialised medical instruments.

Dr Smith selects some instruments the health clinic could use and asks for a quote for the individual instruments. Bill Turnbull quotes the prices of each instrument and tells her that other medical centres have purchased these instruments.

After being told the price of the instruments, which she considers reasonable she asks for them to be ordered for the clinic. Bill Turnbull thanks her for the order and leaves the clinic.

Later in the morning Dr Smith is visited by her business partner, Dr Rose Thompson.

After going over the workload for the next few days they decide to have a coffee break. After preparing the coffee they sit with their cups at a table in the corner of the room.

Once settled Linda then tells Rose Thomson about the visit by the salesman Bill Turnbull and the instruments she has ordered for the clinic. Dr Smith said she was quite impressed by the businesslike manner of the salesman. She went on to say with a twinkle in her eye that he was quite dishy and was quite taken by his soft Inverness-shire accent. Dr Thomson, with a smile, said, "It seems you are quite taken with this man."

After discussing the treatment they were giving to some of their clients, Dr Thomson left to return to her own room before her next client was due to arrive.

When Bill Turnbull next visited Dr Smith at the health clinic he was able to see her without any fuss.

After discussing with her the delivery of the residue of her original order, Bill Turnbull changed the subject and asked Dr Smith what she did in her spare time. Although taken aback by his enquiry she said she enjoyed country walks and going to the theatre to see popular plays. After her reply Bill Turnbull said, "I hope you don't mind me being forward, but would you like to go to the Playhouse next week?" He added that he had been given two complimentary tickets for the show next Friday evening, and would she like to go with him to the show? Dr Smith was taken aback but recovered and was pleased with his proposal as she quite fancied him.

She smiled at him and said, "I would like to go and see the show at the Playhouse, just let me look at my diary." After quickly looking at it she said that she would be free that evening, so what would be the arrangements? "Do I have to meet you at the Playhouse?"

Quite pleased, Bill Turnbull said, "If you give me your address I will pick you up at seven o'clock and drive you to the Playhouse. We can have a drink before we see the show."

Dr Smith was quite impressed and replied, "That would be excellent. My address is 6 Fountainbridge Way, do you know how to get there?"

Bill Turnbull was quick to answer: "I know the Fountainbridge area very well as I have friends who live in that area. Is it far from the old dance hall?" She replied that it was quite close to it. It is only two streets along from the old dance hall on the west side. Bill added, "That's good I will see you on the Friday evening, until then cheerio."

Linda Smith was quite elated with being asked to go out on a date as she hadn't been out with any young man for a long time.

She thought about walking along to her colleague Rose Thomson's room and tell her about her date, but decided to wait until after Friday evening's date and then tell her how she enjoyed the evening.

On the Friday after finishing his calls to some of the firms he dealt with Bill Turnbull drove to his flat in Meadowbank in the late afternoon. He had a shower and after a sandwich and some coffee watched a couple of television programmes.

About six o'clock he had another coffee and then selected a smart shirt to go with his expensive suit. He dressed and then walked down the drive to his Jaguar car parked nearby. Then he drove off to the Fountainbridge area to pick up Dr Smith. It took him about ten minutes to get to the place where she lived as there was some hold-ups with traffic going through Edinburgh.

Arriving at Fountainbridge he parked his car near the flat. It took him only a couple of minutes to walk to it. On reaching her flat he rang the bell and within a short time Linda opened the door. She was dressed in a two-piece blue costume. He hair was drawn back and held in a pony tail with a colourful band.

Bill looked at her, surprised to see how glamorous she was standing in the entrance to the flat. After recovering his composure he said, "You look gorgeous, Linda. It is a proud man who is taking you to the Playhouse tonight."

Linda, quite taken with his remark said, "Thank you, kind sir, for your compliment. I shall just grab my handbag and we can be on our way." She soon returned with her handbag and slammed the outer door and took his arm.

They walked the short distance to his Jaguar and he let her in it first before climbing in himself.

After settling in her seat Linda remarked with a smile, "I hope you didn't steal it so as to impress me tonight."

Bill replied, saying, "Cheeky thing! No, I bought it out of the settlement in my uncle's will."

Bill Turnbull drove off and soon arrived at the parking place for the car which was in one of the side streets near the theatre.

They walked arm in arm to the Playhouse Theatre to see the show Bill had tickets for that evening. After an enjoyable evening seeing the show Bill and Linda walked back to the car. He then drove the car back to the parking place near her flat. They both walked up to the flat.

At the entrance to her flat, Linda turned around and said,

"Thank you so much for a lovely evening and the show was excellent."

Bill said to her, "I hope you don't think I am too forward, but would you like to go out for dinner next week?"

Linda, feeling in a good mood after seeing such a good show and having enjoyed his company, said, "Yes, I would like to go out with you again.

Bill replied, "Shall I pick you up at the same time next Friday?"

Linda answered, "Yes, I will be looking forward to it."

Bill kissed her goodnight and she went into her flat. He could hear her humming a tune from the show. He walked the short distance to where his car was parked and drove back to his own flat in Meadowbank.

Bill picked up Linda at her flat the next Friday and drove to an upmarket restaurant. During their dinner Bill impressed Linda with his knowledge of wines when he selected a particular one to have with a starter and one to have with their main meal.

Linda remarked that she was impressed with his knowledge of wines. Bill replied that he gained the knowledge of wines when he was first employed by a wine import and export firm. What he said was a fib as his first job was a loader in a Cash and Carry firm in Leith. To impress people at dinner he had read a number of books on wines which gave advice on what wines were recommended for various meals. After their dinner at the restaurant Bill drove her back to her flat. This time she invited him in for coffee.

So started a relationship that went on for many weeks.

Although he enjoyed Linda's company Bill, being young and with a roving eye, didn't want a permanent relationship. He selfishly enjoyed the chase and charming young vulnerable women into a relationship and sometimes seduction.

He didn't seem to care if he let these women down when he ended every relationship. He was quite content to continue the relationship with Linda although he didn't really have any fondness for her.

Chapter Two

His opportunity to try another pasture new came along several weeks later.

Linda Smith told Bill on one of the nights together that she could not see him for a short while. She had already arranged to attend a medical course in London. This would mean that she would be away for about two weeks. Still she would telephone him while she was on the course.

Shortly after Linda Smith had left to attend her course in London Bill Turnbull's opportunity to stray off the straight and narrow occurred. He was called into the health clinic so that some medical supplies could be ordered. This time when he arrived at the health clinic he was asked by the receptionist to see the other doctor, Rose Thomson.

Bill Turnbull walked along the corridor and, taking a minute to find the doctor's room, knocked at the door. He had to wait a little while before the door was opened. He could see that she was a little perturbed when she asked him into her room.

She said, "I am sorry I didn't open the door right away but I had a report to finish for a client and it was difficult to write a clear conclusion to the case. Will you please sit down? I am pleased you came so promptly because we have run out of some medical items we are constantly using each day."

After Bill Turnbull sat down, Dr Thomson walked to her desk and sat down. After getting settled she looked him over and was curious to know what sort of person was sitting there.

After some casual conversation she started to weigh up this salesman, as she hadn't seen him when he had previously visited Dr Smith on several occasions in the last few months.

She was quite taken by his smart expensive suit and his soft pleasant Scottish accent. He noticed that she was attracted to his appearance and she blushed when he looked at her for some time.

After taking details of her order for the medical items he said that he would order these items urgently. "You should get some of the items tomorrow and the rest in a couple of days. The firm always keep a good stock of these items especially as they are ordered quite regularly," he said.

Just before he left her room he said, "I hope you don't mind me being forward but I have two complimentary tickets for the Kings Theatre where there is a well-known play being staged." This was his usual fib again. If she agreed he would have to go quickly to the theatre and buy the tickets.

Rose Thomson was taken aback by his request but quickly recovered and said she would like to go to the Kings Theatre with him.

He said the tickets were for the next Friday night if she could make it that night. She said, "I will be free next Friday and would like to go with you to the theatre. In fact it is staging a play I had fancied to see but didn't want to go on my own." She would not have gone with him if she knew that her colleague Linda Smith was in a serious relationship with the salesman.

After she had agreed to go to the theatre with him he said, "Would you like me to collect you at your home, I could pick you up with my car at six p.m. and we could have a drink at the theatre before the play starts?"

She replied, "That would be fine I live in at a flat in a street off Queensferry Road. It will be awkward to get to as there is a one-way system in that area. Look, I will draw you a map of the area with the one-way streets marked." She quickly drew the map and gave it to him.

After he left the health clinic he went right back to his firm's office and ordered up the medical items urgently to satisfy the day-to-day needs of the health clinic.

Once he had completed the order and checked mail that had been left for him by the firm's assistant he locked up his office and walked to his car and drove into Edinburgh and parked in a suitable place near the city centre.

After having a coffee in a nearby Costa coffee shop he walked to the Kings Theatre only a short distance from the shop.

He approached the booking office expecting to purchase two reasonably priced seats for the Friday night play. When he asked the booking clerk for tickets for the Friday night play the clerk looked at him in surprise. She said that all the seats in the theatre for Friday evening had been sold out a while ago. In fact the rest of the week's showing had been sold out. "This play and the actors in it are so popular."

Bill Turnbull was taken aback as he had told Dr Thomson that he had complimentary tickets for the Friday night play.

"Wait a minute," she said, "I've just remembered I've only this morning had two tickets returned for Friday night's play. They are the best seats in the theatre but it would cost you £50 for each ticket.

Bill Turnbull breathed in deeply, knowing he was stuck with the situation he had caused by inviting Dr Thomson to go, with the promise of complimentary tickets to the theatre on the Friday night. He stumped up the £100 for the tickets and left the booking office without saying thank -you to the clerk.

For once his lying had caught up with him and had made a hole in his pocket!

Chapter Three

On the Friday evening Bill Turnbull drove his car to Queensferry Road. After looking at the map Dr Thomson had given him he soon found her flat. It was on the end of the street where there was a steep slope.

Leaving the car he climbed the slope. With the flat being exposed at the top of the slope Dr Thomson could see him from her front window. By the time he reached her front door she came out and closed the door.

She was dressed in a pale blue two-piece suit which set off her slim figure. When Bill Turnbull saw her at the door he said she looked gorgeous. She smiled and took his arm and walked with him to the car. He drove the car to a parking place near the theatre and they went into the theatre's bar for a drink.

While they were sitting having their drink, Dr Thomson noticed the house full sign over the door opposite the bar. She remarked to Bill Turnbull, "You were fortunate getting tickets as I notice the house full sign."

Bill Turnbull was a bit taken aback by her comment but soon recovered and said his boss had good connections with the theatre's management.

Finishing their drinks, Bill Turnbull led Dr Thomson up to the side balcony seats. Dr Thomson, seeing how plush and well spaced out the seats were arranged said, "Your boss must have a very good connection with the theatre's management."

Bill Turnbull, embarrassed by the deception, quickly changed the conversation and talked about the content of the play that he had read about.

After the play finished, with the audience giving the actors a standing ovation, they walked out of the theatre and strolled to where the car was parked. Bill Turnbull drove back to her flat. Before going into her flat she thanked him for a most enjoyable evening. Before kissing her goodnight he asked her if she would like to go out for dinner the following Wednesday evening.

Being in a good mood after seeing such an excellent play and Bill Turnbull being excellent company, she said she would love to go out for dinner with him on the Wednesday.

On leaving her as she went into her flat he walked down the slope with a spring in his step. He had made another conquest. So another relationship was being set up by him despite his affair with her partner Dr Smith. To him it was just part of having a good time while you are young.

The next week Bill Turnbull took Dr Thomson out for dinner at a secluded hotel on the outskirts of Edinburgh.

Chapter Four

On the following Monday Linda Smith had returned from her course in London and rang Bill Turnbull from her flat as she would not be going to the health clinic until the next day.

"Hello Bill, just to let you know I am back from London."

In reply Bill Turnbull asked her how the course in London had gone. "Was it all work and no play?"

"No, it was an interesting course and some parts of the course gave me some proposals that I could use in future at the health clinic. But it wasn't all work; I did see some of the sights in London. I especially enjoyed going to Madam Tussauds and the Houses of Parliament."

Bill Turnbull said, "London sounded very interesting; how about telling me about your sightseeing over drinks? When are you free?"

Dr Smith replied, "Yes how about Wednesday? Could you pick me up at seven o'clock?"

Bill replied, "Sorry, I can't make Wednesday [he already had a date with Rose Thomson that evening]; how about Friday evening I could pick you up at your flat at seven o'clock?"

Linda replied, "That would be fine. I have a lot of work to catch up on this week at the health clinic. I am looking forward to seeing you again, two weeks away from you seems a very long time."

Chapter Five

And so for the next few months Bill Turnbull continued to have dates with Linda Smith and Rose Thomson. Bill Turnbull was able to keep up the deception of the two-timing with the partners for a very long time as both Dr Smith and Dr Thomson kept their personal lives very private.

Sometimes when he was out dining with one of the doctors he would, in error, mention the other doctor's name, but was shrewd enough to change the conversation quickly to avoid it being found out that he was involved with the other doctor.

After going out with Bill Turnbull on numerous occasions Linda Smith asked him why he chose mainly to go to the Barnton Hotel and for drinks in a bar along Leith Walk. "What about trying some other hotel for a change like the Balmoral Hotel in Princes Street? It's the hotel that Rose Thomson goes to sometimes," she said.

Bill was silent for a minute while he racked his brain to come up with a reasonable answer for not picking another hotel for their dinner out. At last he said, "I prefer the Barnton Hotel as it has such good choices of dishes for dinner and their selection of wines is better than the other hotels."

To ensure that he didn't cause clashes with the separate dates with the two doctors he kept a marked-up diary in his office to ensure that he didn't slip up. He meticulously checked the diary from time to time, especially when he had to change a particular date if his business needs meant he had to be away from the district for several days.

Bill Turnbull managed to keep up his double dealing for a couple more months, but after a while, although he enjoyed the intrigue of the two affairs, he was getting worried with the arrangements.

He was spending too much of his salary on entertaining his girlfriends as the two doctors thought he was well off as he boasted about the money his uncle left him, and they allowed him to pay for the dining out. Actually he had spent all his money from his uncle's estate but his ego caused him to pay for the entertainment.

With the affairs lasting so long both Linda and Rose were getting too serious about him and had marriage in mind.

Chapter Six

Sometimes one or other of the doctors would insist on going out on a specific evening. This meant he had to make up more and more excuses for not seeing one of them on that particular evening. Sometimes he even pretended he had to go away on business with his firm.

Again his diary came in handy to get his plans right so that he was able to be ready for their personal demands.

It went well until Bill Turnbull was visiting the health clinic one day accidentally bumped into a patient called Grace Paterson who was about to leave the clinic. With Bill Turnbull's heavy weight hitting her, she slipped onto the floor and felt a pain in her knee. She recovered and stood up, a bit shaken.

Bill Turnbull caught hold of her as she stood up and said, "Sorry I hope I didn't hurt you."

"No I am all right, my knee is a bit sore but it isn't that bad," she said.

Bill Turnbull who always had a roving eye noticed that the person was young, well dressed and good-looking, with a slim figure.

Bill Turnbull said, "I was just leaving after completing my business with Dr Smith – do you have far to go? I have my car outside, could I offer you a lift?"

Grace Paterson was at first hesitant but said, "Thank you,

I was going to hire a taxi to take me to Waverley Station. Surely it will be out of your way?"

Bill Turnbull replied, "No, I have some business to follow up at a firm near Princes Street. I am being rude I should introduce myself. My name is Bill Turnbull and I work for a medical supply firm that supplies this health clinic and have done so for many years."

She shook hands with him and said, "I am Grace Paterson and you can guess I am a patient at this health clinic."

While they were walking to Bill Turnbull's car, Grace looked sideways at Bill Turnbull. She found him quite attractive and appreciated the smart business-like suit he was wearing. She guessed that he was a few years older than her. She was twenty-seven years old but looked younger.

Once they reached the Jaguar, Bill Turnbull let her into it first. She appreciated this gesture and the quality of the car.

On the way to Waverley Station they chatted and Bill found out she was single and seemingly available.

On reaching the station Bill parked the car and let Grace out to catch her train. Bill said to Grace, "I know this is a chance meeting, but would you like to go out one evening for drinks?"

Grace Paterson was a little surprised but being attracted to the man said, "Yes, I would like to go out with you. How about Wednesday evening?"

Bill Turnbull had to think quickly as he already had arranged to meet Rose Thomson on that Wednesday and Linda Smith on the Friday. He replied, "I can't make Wednesday but how about Thursday evening?"

Grace Paterson replied, "That would be fine, I live in

South Queensferry so I would have to travel to Edinburgh to meet you."

Bill Turnbull replied, "If you give me your address I could drive to your house and pick you up there. We could pick a hotel near South Queensferry to go for drinks."

She replied"That would be fine. My address is 14 South Way; it is close to the South Queensferry Station and then we could pick a hotel to go to for drinks. Would seven o'clock suit you?"

Bill Turnbull said, "Yes, that would be fine, I'm looking forward to seeing you."

On the Thursday evening Bill Turnbull drove his Jaguar to South Queensferry and easily found the street where Grace Paterson lived. Bill approached the house which was a small semi-detached villa halfway up South Way.

He knocked at the front door, and Grace opened it and invited him in as she said that she was not quite ready but would only take a couple of minutes. While he was waiting Bill looked around the room and surrounding area and noticed it was tastefully decorated and fitted with modern furniture.

Just before they went out of the house Bill asked Grace why she had chosen to live at South Queensferry. She replied that when she first started to work in Edinburgh she looked at small houses and flats in and around the city but found the price of property too high and her salary was not big enough to afford buying in the Edinburgh area. Although she had some money saved up she looked elsewhere and found the small semi-detached villa in South Queensferry suited her finances. Even though the house was a good distance from Edinburgh, the train service from

South Queensferry was every half an hour and the office she worked in was only a short walk from Waverley Station.

Grace went into the bathroom and after a few minutes said, "There I am ready, where will we go to for a drink?"

Bill Turnbull replied, "What about going to the hotel just across the Forth Road Bridge in North Queensferry? It has a comfortable lounge and is not too busy on a Thursday evening. I've visited it with clients recently who were not disappointed with the hotel."

They walked to Bill's Jaguar and after letting her into the car he drove off over the Forth Road Bridge to the chosen hotel in North Queensferry. On reaching the hotel Bill escorted Grace inside and entered the lounge from the foyer at the side of the hotel.

On settling down in the lounge which was quiet with only one couple sitting at the other end of it, Bill ordered drinks. Grace, looking around, said she was quite impressed with the place and would take her local friends there one evening.

During their conversation Bill found out that Grace ran a small printing business that had been left to her in an old aunt's will when she died two years ago. Grace's parents had died at an early age when she was in her early twenties.

Bill found Grace very easy to talk to and they were able to converse on many topics.

After spending a couple of hours enjoying each other's company Bill took Grace back to her home.

They arranged to meet in Edinburgh the next week as Bill said he would buy tickets for a show at the King's Theatre.

When Bill visited the King's Theatre booking office he

found out that tickets for the show were only available for the Friday night. The booking clerk recognised him and with a cheeky look said, "Do you want the £50 seats again?" Bill accepted the dig from the clerk and laughed, saying, "No, the ones for the stalls would be fine" and paid for two tickets.

After contacting Grace, Bill said to her that he could only get tickets for the Friday evening show at the King's Theatre.

Grace said, "That will be fine I shall work late at the office and just have a couple of sandwiches for my meal, then I will make my way down Leith Walk and meet you at the King's Theatre. Would seven o'clock be a suitable time to meet? If that is all right we could have a drink in the bar before the start of the show."

Chapter Seven

Now Bill had a problem as he usually saw Linda Smith on a Friday evening. So he had to telephone her and ask her if they could change their date to a Saturday. His excuse was that he had urgent business with a firm he usually obtained specialised medical equipment for in Dundee.

The next Friday evening Bill met Grace at the King's Theatre and they had a drink in the bar before going into the theatre. Both enjoyed the show. Coming out of the theatre, Bill hailed a taxi which took them to Waverley Station. Before Grace took the train to South Queensferry they agreed to meet again the following week.

Soon Bill was having a relationship with Grace. After getting to know Grace quite well he ended up making constant visits to her house.

Bill was able to continue the affair with Grace without detection for a long time. This was mainly because South Queensferry was quite a distance from Edinburgh. It was very unlikely they would be seen by his friends or colleagues as it was not a place they would visit for a night out. Moreover, the doctors always visited Edinburgh hotels or bars for nights out.

With trying to satisfy his relationships with the two doctors and now wanting to see Grace more often he had to make more excuses to Rose and Linda.

For a while this worked out reasonably well, but gradually both Linda and Rose were becoming more possessive and wanted to see Bill more often.

Chapter Eight

Unfortunately things came to a head after Bill had been seeing Grace on many of the evenings over the following weeks.

It was Linda who nearly caught Bill out. She had arranged to see Bill on a Wednesday evening but had thought she had to meet him on the Tuesday evening.

All dressed up for the evening, she took her car and travelled to his flat off Queen Street. After knocking at his door for several minutes in exasperation she was ready to return to her own flat.

Just before she left the flat a neighbour came out from a nearby flat and asked Linda if she was looking for Mr Turnbull. Linda turned around at the neighbour and said, "Yes, we were supposed to be going out together for a drink in a bar in Princes Street but he seems to be out." "Well," the neighbour said, "Mr Turnbull left his flat about half an hour ago and was nicely dressed in a smart suit; it must have been something special to be so well dressed."

What had actually happened was that Bill had left to meet Linda's colleague Rose Thomson for dinner in the West End.

Linda felt she had been stood up and was quite angry and strutted off to pick up her car at the end of the street.

When she returned to her own flat she had a large drink of her favourite whisky to calm herself down.

After finishing her drink she casually picked up her diary. Thumbing through the pages she discovered that she had made a mistake with the evening she had arranged to see Bill. They had decided to meet on Wednesday, not Tuesday evening.

She felt much better after finding out about her error in getting the day wrong for meeting Bill, but a glimmer of suspicion crept into her thoughts.

She wondered what Bill was doing that evening going out all dressed up. It didn't seem like he was on a business appointment. Linda decided that she would test Bill to see if he was two-timing her.

After their evening out on the Wednesday, Linda asked to see Bill on the following Tuesday to allay the suspicion that he could be seeing someone else on that evening. Bill started to make excuses that were not very plausible and was taken aback by Linda pushing him to agree to going out with her on the following Tuesday evening.

He reluctantly agreed to a date on that evening before saying goodnight to her. So next day Bill had to do some quick talking on the telephone to his girlfriend Grace. He asked her to change their date to a Thursday after she said she had other plans for the Wednesday.

Then he had to telephone Rose and ask her to change their date from Thursday to a Wednesday. When the changes were fixed he sat in his office where he made the calls and sighed with relief. He felt that it had been a close call. Although their date on the Tuesday went smoothly and she hadn't caught him out, Linda still felt Bill was dating someone else.

So she kept changing the dates for seeing him in the

succeeding weeks which caused him much confusion as the other two girlfriends started to make objections to him constantly changing their dates.

In those weeks with all the changes to dates caused by Linda, Bill had to resort to making up excuses such as having to have meetings with business clients or saying he had a bad cold.

This made all three girlfriends suspicious as he seemed to recover quickly enough for the next date.

Bill had to make so many changes as a result of Linda opting for different evenings out that he finally made a mistake.

He made arrangements to see Linda on the following Thursday but made a mistake when he put their date in his diary as Wednesday. When he saw Rose that week he had made arrangements to see her on the Thursday, having checked his diary that day and hadn't noticed his mistake. He had arranged to see her at his flat at seven o'clock.

Linda arrived at his flat before seven o'clock as she had a habit of being early for their dates.

Rose who had a habit of being late arrived at ten past seven and knocked on the door of Bill's flat. Bill opened the door and when he saw Rose he realised that he had double dated and went pale with fright. He came outside the flat and tried to put Rose off, saying it was the wrong day.

Too late, Linda, hearing a voice she recognised, came to the door and saw Rose smartly dressed to go out for the evening. Linda now knew her suspicions were realised and Bill had been two-timing her by dating Rose as well as herself.

Turning to Bill, Rose said, "You double-crossing rat,"

and struck him across the face with her hand. Bill had only time enough to put his hand up to his face to feel the pain when Linda poured the gin and tonic over his head.

Linda shouted at Bill, "You won't see me again, Bill, I agree with Rose — you are a double-crossing rat." She picked up her coat and walked out of the flat, soon to be followed by Rose who turned around and made her way to her own car.

Chapter Nine

So ended Bill's escapades with the two doctors. Now Bill was left to straighten out his private life and be faithful, we hope, to Grace Paterson. Only time will tell if he has learnt his lesson with the two doctors.

A few weeks after the incident at Bill Turnbull's flat and with the health clinic quiet, Rose strolled along to Linda's room for a chat.

After talking about the incident at Bill's flat and their embarrassment at being duped by Bill, Rose brought up the subject of Bill not coming back to the health clinic on business matters since the incident. Linda said, "Maybe he is too embarrassed to confront us again."

About a couple of weeks later a young attractive young man entered the health clinic and approached the receptionist.

She asked him, "How can I help you?" The young man told her he was Jim Muir and had taken over the handling of the medical equipment business from Bill Turnbull.

The receptionist who was always inquisitive asked him, "What has happened to Bill Turnbull?" Jim Muir answered "He asked his boss for a transfer to another area!"

The receptionist said to the salesman, "You are lucky; with a number of patients finishing their treatment today, we are fairly quiet. The two doctors are chatting in Dr Smith's room so I can take you along to her room so you can see Dr Smith and Dr Thomson at the same time.

So the receptionist led him along the corridor to Dr Smith's room and knocked at her door.

When Dr Smith opened the door the receptionist with a knowing glance at the salesman and aware of what had transpired with the double dating said, "This is Jim Muir who has taken over from Bill Turnbull," and then left the room.

Both doctors welcomed Jim Muir into the room and sat him down. They noticed Jim Muir was young, tall, good-looking and well dressed in a smart suit.

The doctors could not help fancying Jim Muir as he was so attractive. After some small talk, Jim Muir was given some orders for medical equipment. Saying goodbye, he left the room with a charming smile and his business card.

After he had gone the doctors looked at each other. Linda began to comment on Jim Muir's good looks but stopped herself and said, "No not again! We won't encourage young commercial travellers ever again!"

Rose replied, "I wholeheartedly agree with you. We shall keep our dealings on a strictly business footing."

Despite their agreement, both of them sighed, remembering the good times they had with Bill Turnbull.